Layman's Bible Book Commentary
Acts

LAYMAN'S BIBLE BOOK COMMENTARY

ACTS

VOLUME 19

Robert L. Maddox, Jr.

BROADMAN PRESS
Nashville, Tennessee

My deepest gratitude to my wife, Linda,
and our children for their constant love,
encouragement, and support;

to the congregation of First Baptist
Church, Calhoun, Georgia, who have
been the ears and mirrors of the ideas
in this book;

to D. P. Brooks of the Sunday
School Board for his willingness to
help me free some angels within;

to Wanda Shaw, the world's most dedicated,
diligent, and patient secretary.

Dewey Decimal Classification: 226.6
Subject heading: BIBLE. N. T. ACTS
Library of Congress Catalog Card Number: 78–67926
Printed in the United States of America

Foreword

The *Layman's Bible Book Commentary* in twenty-four volumes was planned as a practical exposition of the whole Bible for lay readers and students. It is based on the conviction that the Bible speaks to every generation of believers but needs occasional reinterpretation in the light of changing language and modern experience. Following the guidance of God's Spirit, the believer finds in it the authoritative word for faith and life.

To meet the needs of lay readers, the *Commentary* is written in a popular style, and each Bible book is clearly outlined to reveal its major emphases. Although the writers are competent scholars and reverent interpreters, they have avoided critical problems and the use of original languages except where they were essential for explaining the text. They recognize the variety of literary forms in the Bible, but they have not followed documentary trails or become preoccupied with literary concerns. Their primary purpose was to show what each Bible book meant for its time and what it says to our own generation.

The Revised Standard Version of the Bible is the basic text of the *Commentary*, but writers were free to use other translations to clarify an occasional passage or sharpen its effect. To provide as much interpretation as possible in such concise books, the Bible text was not printed along with the comment.

Of the twenty-four volumes of the *Commentary*, fourteen deal with Old Testament books and ten with those in the New Testament. The volumes range in pages from 140 to 168. Four major books in the Old Testament and five in the New are treated in one volume each. Others appear in various combinations. Although the allotted space varies, each Bible book is treated as a whole to reveal its basic message with some passages getting special attention. Whatever plan of Bible study the reader may follow, this *Commentary* will be a valuable companion.

Despite the best-seller reputation of the Bible, the average survey of Bible knowledge reveals a good deal of ignorance about it and its primary meaning. Many adult church members seem to think that its study is intended for children and preachers. But some of the newer translations have been making the Bible more readable for all ages. Bible study has branched out from Sunday into other days of the week, and into neighborhoods rather than just in churches. This *Commentary* wants to meet the growing need for insight into all that the Bible has to say about God and his world and about Christ and his fellowship.

BROADMAN PRESS

Contents

Introduction:

The Surprise in Perspective

The church happened. That's just the fact of the matter. No *person* set out to create the church. In fact, the world knew nothing of the church, had no notion of such an institution, and surely felt no need for another religious superstructure. But the church happened through a series of marvelous surprises along the way. Some of the surprises can be explained in terms of a combination of sociology and psychology, while other surprises have their origin in heaven itself.

Of course, the church was not an accident. It had been part of God's grand design for his people from the beginning. Looking down across the centuries, God could foresee the creation and establishment of the church; but he chose to wait until the world was hurting badly enough before he gave reality, concretion to his plan for the church. Not only the clock time (*chronos*) had to be right; the fullness of time (*kairos*) had to be right before he would set in motion the marvelous life and events that would eventually give birth to the church.

The men and women who accompanied Jesus during his ministry around the Sea of Galilee and into the exotic, impressive, ancient city of Jerusalem had no notion at all of their participation in the birth process of God's new community. Along the way Jesus had tried to give his close friends clues about what he was doing, but they were too enamored with him and too wrapped up in themselves to hear what he was saying to them. After all, who needed a church (whatever that was) when they had the gorgeous Temple in Jerusalem and neighborhood synagogues throughout the country!

One of the exciting dimensions of our discipleship of the living Lord is that we often do participate in events whose meaning and results we do not perceive except from the vantage point of a spiritually informed hindsight.

So we say that the church happened but was was no accident. Begone any silly hypothesis that a group of frustrated disciples mourning the untimely death of their leader entered into a conspiracy to create an institution that would perpetuate his memory. Because the disciples were a willing lot and because they truly loved their risen Lord, God entered into their individual and communal life in an altogether unique way to take part in the birth of his church.

Not only did this group of followers *not* intend to found a new institution; they did not want to leave the religious patterns of their forefathers. Indeed, in the early stages of sorting out new meanings for their lives, they would have been horrified to hear a proposal that the church would replace synagogue and Temple. They loved the Temple. They were comfortable in their synagogues. They knew their way around in the liturgy. The patterns of worship were as familiar as the trails among their villages. The thought forms were ingrained from centuries of nearly unchanged routine. Alter or challenge those venerable institutions? Never!

But the new did explode.

As we make our way through this commentary, you will be able to feel that newness with Peter, Paul, Barnabas, and the others. These early leaders were mortal and subject to all the trials and tribulations of the flesh. They got hurt and bled, grew discouraged, and, from time to time, flung down their hats in anger just like you and I do. Give those early disciples their due for being willing to risk all and follow Jesus; but do not make them little gods or little saviors. They were men and women. But—and this is an important qualification— they were increasingly willing to be led by the Spirit, to risk life, limb, and fortune to do what they felt the risen Lord was moving them to do. It was no less expensive for Peter to give up his boats and nets and follow after Jesus than it would be for you to close the doors of your shop or office and become a traveling preacher.

As we go along, try to "flesh out" these people we meet. Feel their shock and surprise and overwhelming sense of *newness* as the Spirit of God became a mighty everyday force in their lives. If we can gather up all these new and human events into a total experience, we can at least approximate the adventure that runs through the entire book of Acts.

Before we begin the study of the book, let's have a quick look at the basic information about Acts.

There is little doubt but that the author of the Gospel of Luke and the author of Acts are one and the same. It would be beyond the scope of this book to go into the details of the debate concerning the authorship of Acts; but if you would like to explore such a question, a good Bible encyclopedia or a more technical commentary would provide interesting reading.

There are some grand traditions concerning Luke, but the Bible itself is agonizingly silent about this literary giant. Some say he was originally from Antioch and had met Paul in that city, but only in Troas (where the "we" narrative picks up) did they strike up the bargain to travel together. We do know beyond reasonable doubt that he was a Gentile physician and that he did travel with Paul the rest of the apostle's active ministry. From his writings and the few brief references to him, we get the picture of a brilliant, steady, precise, spiritual man to whom faith in Jesus Christ was as real as the morning's sunrise and just as beautiful. Scholars differ as to the date of Acts, but many feel that both Luke and Acts came after the fall of Jerusalem in A.D. 70. Acts may have been written about A.D. 75–80.

Though the book pulsates with life, it is nonetheless a carefully constructed document. Writing out of his background as a Greek and as a physician, Luke paid attention to important details and carefully footnoted when he deemed it necessary. When he was not an eyewitness to events such as Pentecost, the activity of Philip, and the death of Stephen, he sought out eyewitnesses to get a full-orbed picture of what did happen. Indeed, while Paul languished in prison along the way—especially the more than two years he spent in Caesarea—Luke probably spent his time talking with people, including Mary, the mother of Jesus, about the events in the life of Jesus and the activities of the believers before he came on the scene. When you read Acts, you can be confident that you are reading a Holy Spirit-inspired book and a substantial historical document.

The purpose of the book of Acts is to talk about the unimpeded spread of the church throughout the Roman world. Underlying that obvious purpose is Luke's aim to show that this spread took place in the power of the Holy Spirit as the gospel penetrated geographical, social, racial, and religious barriers.

Although the traditional title of the book has been "The Acts of the Apostles," it only lists them before focusing on Peter, John, and James and finally giving way to the aggressive ministry of Paul. Some have called it "The Acts of the Holy Spirit" because the continuing presence of Christ worked through men and women to proclaim and live out the news of God's coming for all the peoples of the world. Even though actual language about the Holy Spirit diminishes as the book progresses, there is little doubt but that the participants in this marvelous drama saw themselves under the sway and leadership of the Holy Spirit of God.

A Series of Surprises

1:1 to 5:42

Getting Ready (1:1-26)

A Moment for Remembering (1:1-5)

Luke told his friend Theophilus (v. 1) that he had written Acts as a continuation of his first book (the Gospel of Luke) for two reasons: Jesus' work did not end with the resurrection, and Luke did not get through telling the story in his first book.

We would love to know more about Theophilus. He must have been Luke's dear friend to have been the official recipient of both of the doctor's literary masterpieces. Some capable scholars have said that Theophilus was no particular person but that the name simply stood for a generalization like "Dear Reader." However, we may prefer to think of him as a real person and as the pillar of some church. With a name that means "dear to God," he must have been born to good parents who wanted to encourage excellent growth in matters of the Spirit.

Unlike some other great religious leaders, Jesus went about *doing* as well as teaching. Luke reminded his friend that in the previous book he had talked about the activity and the words of Jesus. In fact, the acts of Jesus gave credence, validation, authority to what he taught. Some writers have said that Jesus' teachings were not completely original with him, that he sifted through the Old Testament and other Jewish writers to construct the main body of his teaching. Be that as it may, the life he lived, the death he died, and the resurrection he experienced infuse the body of his teachings with the crystal-clear ring of authority. These marvelous, unrepeatable deeds give timelessness, even immortality, to what Jesus said. Indeed, most of our theology is composed of reflections on God's mighty acts in the world. In an attempt to get meaning out of and to preserve some extraordinary deed that God does, we construct our theological statements. The old adage "I had rather see a sermon than hear one" has sure footing in the life of Jesus.

15

Jesus was no frantic activitist running here and there and doing good deeds. The more we understand his life, the more we understand the purpose behind his wonderfully free and unselfish acts. Even in its spontaneity, his ministry had a sense of direction behind it that was designed to communicate truth and the presence of God.

This same attempt at conserving via language the deeds of God through the church characterizes not only the book of Acts but most of the New Testament. Every day brought new surprises, new thrusts, new revelations from the Holy Spirit. As persons attempted to understand the events, the conceptualizing and writing took place.

Luke and Acts, along with the other Gospels, are grand attempts to show the meaning of God's activity in Christ and in the church as well as to perpetuate those deeds for all of history.

The book of Luke ends with the ascension of Jesus (24:50-51). Acts begins with the ascension of Jesus (v. 2). Like any good two-volume work, there is a bit of careful overlapping so that the reader can get his bearings. The connecting overlap is the ascension of Jesus. But before he went back to the Father, he gave commandments to his apostles. Read Luke 24:44-49. In that paragraph Luke recorded the commissioning (commanding) of the apostles. Jesus told them that he must suffer, die, and then rise from the dead; that they were to be preachers and witnesses (hence the word *apostles,* the ones sent by the Lord) of his life, death, and resurrection; that their preaching was to embrace all nations; and that a different visitation of the Holy Spirit would come to enable and empower them in their newly commissioned tasks. Jesus' emphasis on these men always focused on their task or their function rather than a conferring of status. These men were to wait for the coming of the Spirit before they went rushing off to tackle their new assignments.

The writer of Acts included Jesus among the rest of us who speak on the authority of the Holy Spirit. Even though Jesus was resurrected and in his new body, he made it clear that all his utterances and activities were from the Father through the Holy Spirit.

With what bewilderment the eleven must have heard Jesus' last commandments! Their minds were reeling. Every day brought new traumas: the despair of the crucifixion, the excitement, fear, and incredulity of the resurrection, and the no-nonsense orders to go to the Mount of Olives, then up to Galilee and then back to Jerusalem. All that talk from the Master about preaching to the nations must have absolutely overwhelmed those simple men. Probably most of them had never even been out of their tiny country. The idea of going into other nations of a hostile world must have struck terror into their pounding hearts.

They were men who could receive the power of God when it came and remember those ringing words of Jesus, uttered before he ascended back to the Father. In due time they acted out the commands that their Lord had given them.

Some churches have nearly deified the apostles. All have been canonized as official saints. No doubt each of the men rose to exhilarating heights of devotion and achievement in the cause of their Lord. But do not be intimidated by these men from Palestine because each was an ordinary man who was able only after a great deal of soul-searching to fully commit his life to the risen Christ. Nothing they did is beyond our ability. Our problem is not inability or a deficient call. Our problem is the unwillingness to completely surrender our lives to that same Christ.

For forty of the most unusual days that this earth ever experienced, the risen Christ presented himself alive (v. 3). Hundreds, maybe even thousands, had seen him die. To refute his detractors—but even more, to undergird his disciples—the resurrected Jesus conducted a ministry of personal appearances. How many times did he appear? It is hard to know and actually beside the point. He came to the disciples to give them the courage to face trials for his sake. By his words and visibility Jesus assured them that the same God who had snatched him from the bowels of the earth and from the clutches of death would be with them as they lived out their commission to go into all the world.

His message: the kingdom of God. The phrase was quite familiar to the Jews of Jesus' day. They longed for the restoration of the kingdom. Entire parties (often terrorist bands) sprang up advocating, preparing for, and even trying to precipitate the restoration of the kingdom. Of course, what they wanted was a form of the restoration of the Davidic kingdom or at least something of an independent state such as the Maccabees had created during the second century B.C. But their concept of the kingdom missed God's intention. Through Christ God was bringing into reality a mental and spiritual mind-set in which God's sovereign power could be plainly and consistently lived out in the hearts and nations of men. It was this kind of kingdom, this type of spiritual climate, that Jesus wanted to bring about. And it was to this kingdom army that he called his apostles and ultimately his church.

The apostles, the products of their own times, had to work through their initial disappointment when they saw thrones and royal trappings slipping away from them. They had to accept into their own thought patterns the larger, expanded, and universal kingdom that Jesus insistently preached. It was not an easy transition. Even after the life-changing experiences that occurred at Pentecost, it took years for them to sufficiently internalize Jesus' concept of the kingdom of God.

Jesus spoke to the disciples "while staying with them" (v. 4). One translation reads, "while in bivouac with them." The army is poised for the big battle. The night before the penultimate conflict is to begin, the commanding general leaves his headquarters in the rear of the camp and bivouacs with the troops. From campfire to pup tent he strolls, encouraging, inspiring, answering questions, giving them clues about his strategy, and building up their morale for the baptism of fire and bloodshed that surely awaits them at the breaking of dawn. The general snacks from their plain mess, even though he has no need for food at all. He has no illusions about what the morning will bring. Because he loves these men with all his being, he wants them to meet their day bravely, a credit to themselves, to his own leadership, and to the grand banner under which they march.

Jesus bivouaced with the apostles for those forty days. Coming and going. Eating with them. Hunching down around their campfires. Appearing in the midst of their hushed conferences. Yes, laughing and joking with them. Saying in it all: Take heart, little band. You are about to embark on the grandest adventure in all of human history. I have chosen you to speak to kings and governors. You will sail through stormy seas to the ends of this world. You will be sorely tested, and most of you will die a martyr's death because of your steadfastness. But be of good cheer. I have literally given you the keys to heaven and earth. I will invigorate you with the very power of the universe. Empires and idolatries will tremble, crumble, and fall before your gentle but firm revolution. You will say and do things that never in your wildest imaginings would you have believed possible or yourselves capable of performing. Have no fear of the dawn. It ultimately holds only triumph for you.

But for now, take your rest. Get your bearings. Go to Jerusalem for a few days of last-minute preparations and resource gathering. Spend the time in prayer—expectant prayer—because something never seen in the world before is about to manifest itself. You will need to be ready to receive the experience when it comes to you.

A brand-new kind of baptism is revealed in verse 5. The Jews knew about baptism, for the rite had been part of their religious heritage for centuries. Part of the process by which a Gentile converted to Judaism was baptism. John came baptizing, and most likely some of the apostles had received his baptism or at least had witnessed the rite from a riverbank. But Jesus was trying to prepare them for a new experience, and he used the familiar to introduce the unfamiliar. They knew about water baptism, in which the person was submerged in a pool or stream. Holy Spirit baptism would have the same form, but the spiritual aftereffects would not evaporate as water did off the dripping convert.

The Ascension (1:6-11)

Details of the forty days Jesus spent on earth after the resurrection are sketchy. We ache to have a running account of all that must have taken place during those tumultous last weeks of Jesus' ministry on earth, but such full reporting was beyond the scope of the writer's intentions. How did the apostles know to assemble on the Mount of Olives that fateful day? We do not know. But some directive from the risen Jesus must have come.

As they gathered, maybe the men sensed that this was the last time they would see their Lord on the earth. One of them almost breathlessly gave voice to their desperate question: "Lord, will you at this time restore the kingdom of Israel?" (v. 6). "Lord," he pled, speaking for the rest of the anxious apostles, "I know you have told us your kingdom is not of this world, but we have a hard time with that idea. Let me ask you one more time before you go. Is David coming again, or is one of his heirs going to take over the reins of government? Will we hear drums roll and see uniformed armies escort a real king into Jerusalem?" And all the expectations of five hundred years of Jewish pride and hope literally screamed from the man's mouth, even though his tones were hushed.

Gently, ever so gently, Jesus addressed the misput question by not answering the query. Perhaps with a touch of parental weariness in his voice, for the umpteenth time, he suggested again: "My friends, my kingdom is different. Please understand that my kingdom is different."

To the misput question Jesus gave a correct but indirect answer (vv. 7-8). The kingdom he was initiating and in which they would be so prominent was not one of calendar or seasons. A day could be like a thousand years, or a thousand years could be like a day. They were not to concern themselves with the timetable. That sort of thing has always been in the hands of God; and even though anticipating and predicting times and seasons is a fascinating religious hobby, such is not central to worship. During his ministry, Jesus had a way of telling them that he did not keep up with such esoteric notions.

But Jesus did give the disciples a promise of great victory for the kingdom. He said in effect: "What you can expect is a great infilling of the Holy Spirit. You can count on that because in just a short while, when your hearts are ready, you are going to experience a heavenly visitation such as few in the history of the world have ever had."

"And you shall be my witnesses." God through his Spirit has already equipped us to do his work. Those disciples on the hillside had all the native talent and gifts they needed to be witnesses to the ends of the earth. What they lacked was surrender to the Holy Spirit. When the Spirit moved in on them and they chose to yield to him, their innate capacities were freed so that they could do the work which God through Christ had already equipped them to do. They had been in Jesus' school for three years. They would continue to grow and develop through their graduate work in the university of hard knocks, but they already had the essential information.

"Jerusalem and in all Judea and Samaria and to the end of the earth." Jesus was pushing their concept of geography to the limits. They were untraveled men. Jesus himself never left Palestine and its immediate environs, as far as we know. He was urging them to go beyond what they had known both of geography and culture to see the universal implications of the gospel. Not only Jews in the capital city and their native country, but half-breeds in Samaria and outright Gentiles in the farthest reaches of the earth had a stake in the new gospel. It took some dramatic revelations from God to convince the apostles of the universality of the gospel, but Jesus laid the groundwork that day on Mount Olive.

Memory pegs are important. Maybe when Peter had his vision on the rooftop and subsequent encounter with Cornelius the Roman, he harked back to that day on the hillside. "What was it that Jesus said? 'To the ends of the earth'—now I see!"

Before the resurrection Jesus had told them that he would have to go away. His spontaneous and unpredictable postresurrection appearances should have given the disciples the clue that he would not always be visible to them. But after each of those appearances, they probably waited expectantly for him to come again. The ascension (v. 9), surprise that it was, became God's way of saying, "He will not come to you again as the Son of earth. Ring down the curtain on that phase of my plan. Take a brief intermission while the stage is rearranged a bit; then hurry back for the next magnificent act of my epic story of human redemption." After he had finished speaking to them, he was gone from their sight.

Luke alone recorded the ascension; and even between the Gospel and Acts, there is a slight variation as to the exact scenario. Why Luke alone? The physician's neatly organized mind and world outlook would push him to set down on paper what others knew but found unnecessary to write about. Luke carefully recorded the beginning of Jesus' ministry. That ministry would also need a statement of conclusion, which the doctor carefully provided.

Even though the ascension as such was not talked about in other New Testament writings, the church was quickly unanimous in agreeing that Jesus, the risen Son, would forever be seated at the right hand of the Father from whom he had originally "descended." Paul, who did not talk about the ascension, sang in Philippians 2, "wherefore God has highly exalted him . . ."

In verses 10-11 two men in white robes said in effect to the disciples, "He's coming again." Nothing electrified and charged the preaching of the church quite like that. No program was given. Jesus had said only a few moments ago not to fret about the timetable. But none of that is to negate the impact of that incredibly powerful statement: He will return.

Through the centuries, conversation and speculation about the Lord's return have been sources of great confusion. All our debating and even arguing flies directly in the face of the Lord's own caution about getting bogged down in eschatology. We all have our opinions. Great. What matters is that we feel the urgency of our work, that we witness in the full expectation and confidence that he will return someday.

The Acts Begin (1:12-26)

Notice the words that crop up all through the Scripture such as *then, therefore, hitherto, henceforth, but,* and so forth. Often they mark strategic changes of direction in the holy events and/or indicate that the gospel has turned another divinely inspired corner.

Luke said, "Then they returned to Jerusalem" (v. 12). The Lord had gone back to the Father. The men standing by had gently chided the small band for just standing there with their mouths hanging open. Jesus had said for them to go back to Jerusalem and wait.

Imagine the upper room. Tradition identifies this room as the second-floor living room in John Mark's home. Jesus and his disciples had met there for their last supper together. It was from this room that Judas had rushed out to set in motion those dastardly events that led to the death of the Lord. On the couches around the table the disciples disconcertedly lounged while Jesus foretold his death, their own suffering, and their rejection, while at the same time trying to encourage them with the promise of the Spirit and ultimate victory. From this room Jesus and the eleven had walked to the garden, where he would be betrayed not only by Judas but by the eleven themselves who dozed while he agonized and who fled when he was arrested.

It would be natural to return to that room about a half-mile (sabbath day journey) from the hill of ascension in obedience to Jesus' "Return to Jerusalem" order (v. 13). Many large homes had such an upper chamber, either enclosed as a second story or as a rooftop patio. A desire to escape from the heat, to have privacy, and to follow a tradition in architecture combined to create upper rooms all over that part of the world. The hospitality of the owner, Mark and his family or whoever, would encourage their repeated use of the room.

The atmosphere must have been one of fluid emotions. More had happened in the past forty days than they could assimilate. Now this latest incredible surprise—the Lord taken up into the heavens while they looked on! And the order to go to the city and wait. Wait for what? No one was at all sure. No doubt, though, their apprehension was at least balanced by the keenest kind of anticipation. A God who could raise Jesus from the dead, make possible those spontaneous

appearances, and then lift him before their eyes would have no diffi-
culty in continuing the extraordinary.

They were all there: the eleven disciples, Mary, the mother of Jesus,
Jesus' brothers, other women, and an undetermined number of unnamed followers of the Lord (v. 14).

A vast segment of the Christian world makes more of Mary than
the Bible claims and far more than she understood herself to be.
Through the centuries, heated debates have raged over the nature
of the mother of Jesus. We can most assuredly say that she is not
the "Mother of God." She was not virgin born. We stop far short of
canonizing her as a saint and making her equal with the Savior. But
we in the Protestant world have tended to overlook her or to sell
her too short. God would have picked only the best of all women
to be the mother of Jesus. Even as a young woman she must have
possessed the finest of human characteristics for the heavenly Father
to trust her with the rearing of Jesus.

If we believe the incarnation, Jesus was a real person, subject to
all the problems of the flesh. He would need a mother and a father
who could carefully guide him into the knowledge of God, urge him
to channel his best energies, and help him develop the prodigious
talents and abilities that he had evidently begun to exhibit at an early
age. Although details concerning Jesus' years of development are quite
sketchy, we can appreciate the excellent rearing from his parents
that he must have received. Let's not deify Mary, but let's appreciate
her and emulate her as a great mother.

His brothers were present also. No doubt they had had their troubles
with Jesus. It would be difficult for siblings to grow up with someone
like Jesus and not be jealous of him. Our understanding of Jesus would
quickly inform us that he did not engender the rivalry, but it must
have occurred. Then as he left home and gained such instant fame,
their struggles would intensify. Some of his brothers may have been
rather quickly drawn to him as not only brother but also Lord, while
others could not quite admit that their older brother was indeed the
promised one from God. Apparently, however, before the end of his
ministry—or maybe as a result of the resurrection—they all became
believers. Four brothers are mentioned: James, Joses, Judas, and Simon
(Mark 6:3). James became the leader of the church in Jerusalem, and
Judas (not Iscariot) is regarded by some to be the author of Jude.

Some scholars have gone to great lengths to suggest that Jesus had no brothers, that Jesus was Mary's only child. But such a pursuit is unnecessary and unfruitful. It should cause us no problem to believe that after Jesus was born, Mary and Joseph had other children.

If there had been any doubt concerning the leader of the apostles, those days of waiting cleared up the issue forever. Clearly the big fisherman emerged as the spokesman for the group (v. 15). His leadership, however, was earned and assumed, a product of who he was as a person rather than a position conferred on him by Jesus. It is an additional historical inaccuracy to ascribe ongoing leadership to Peter over other Christian leaders such as Paul. Simon Peter was a great leader, a man who vigorously risked himself on behalf of the young church, whose personality was both warm and compelling. But to make him a successor to Christ is going too far.

But meanwhile, back to the upper room. As the days wore on, the idea occurred to the group that Judas ought to be replaced. So Peter stood up in the midst of the group and gave voice to the thought that was going through many minds: Someone should take Judas' place.

In verses 16-19 Peter continued by quoting Psalm 41:9 as a prophecy foretelling Jesus' betrayal by a "bosom friend" who turned out to be Judas. There is debate concerning the exact way that Judas died and how the cemetery came to be purchased. The most popular idea is that when he hanged himself, his body "exploded," causing his organs to burst out. Perhaps the priests took the money they had paid Judas, which he had in his deep remorse flung back at them, and purchased a paupers' field. In that sense, then, Judas purchased the field.

In verse 20 Peter quoted from the Psalms, this time 69:25 and 109:8, and interpreted these texts as mandating another to take Judas' place among the twelve. Judas was replaced not because he died but because he defected. A vacancy created by such an intolerable act would have to be filled in order to maintain the parallel between the twelve disciples and the twelve tribes. On down the line, this parallel would not be maintained as martyrdom took first one and then another of the twelve; but at this early stage of their new life together, there was a felt urgency to fill up the black void left by Judas.

The group set forth standards for a bona fide replacement (vv. 21-22). He must have been a follower of Jesus from the time of John the Baptist, and he must have been a witness to the resurrection. When we apply this narrow standard to apostleship, we conclude that the original twelve were unique unto themselves. However, when we appreciate the broader dimensions of the word, we can apply the term more generally and even call ourselves apostles.

Two men were nominated (v. 23). One was Joseph, whose surname was Barsabbas (son of the sabbath) and who also bore the Latin name Justus. The Scriptures are silent about him, but tradition says that somewhere in his further ministry he was challenged by unbelievers to drink snake's venom in the Lord's name, which he did, and suffered no ill effects.

Matthias was the other candidate. Like his fellow candidate, he emerged from the mists for one brief moment and then faded away again. If tradition is to be believed, though, he was faithful to his calling, preached in Judea, and was finally stoned to death by the Jews. Indeed, Jesus' word to his ambitious disciples to beware of the bitter cup he was offering to them was tragically fulfilled time and again.

Exactly how the two men were "put forward" is not known. Perhaps they were such outstanding men that common consent simply thrust them to the forefront of all other possible candidates. Some texts have Peter naming the two candidates. But regardless of how they came to the ballot, the eleven prayed, voted on the two, and enrolled Matthias among the twelve (vv. 24-26). No doubt the entire company breathed a sigh of relief when the number ordained by the Lord was once again safely rounded out and the blackhearted Judas was replaced by Matthias.

Surprised by the Day of Pentecost (2:1-47)

The Sights and Sounds of Pentecost (2:1-13)

Pentecost (v. 1) is one of the feasts of ancient Judaism that has its roots in Leviticus 23:15-21. Through the years it was variously called the Feast of Weeks or the Feast of Firstfruits and was scheduled to begin at the close of harvesttime. Other traditions have the feast commemorating the giving of the Law on Sinai. It is called Pentecost because it begins on the fiftieth day from the first Sunday after Passover.

Two aspects of the day stand out without any controversy: the day
was Pentecost; and the disciples, apostles, family of Jesus, and others
were together in one place. Several times Luke emphasized the tie
that bound those first Christians. They clung to each other because
there were no others to whom they could turn for support and understanding. Those who had to return to their nearby homes at night
may have remained with their friends as long as they could, left only
reluctantly, and hurried back to the upper room at the first light of
dawn—from fear, uncertainty, and the overwhelming sense of expec-
tancy that pervaded those days of vigil. The day of Pentecost would
have been no exception. The feast had begun at sundown, since that
was the way the Jewish sabbath was calculated. But the first thing
the next morning, the quiet of predawn Jerusalem was disturbed as
dozens of Christians padded toward their headquarters.

Then it happened (v. 2). While they were together, possibly in
prayer for the day, from nowhere, and yet from everywhere, came
one of the most electrifying, galvanizing, and energizing experiences
ever to come to man on this earth. God came. God in the form of
the Holy Spirit came upon the people. Did the curtains sigh under
the weight of the first breath of wind? Did the lamps flicker? Did
strands of their hair rustle like angels' wings? Who knows? But they
would talk about that day for the rest of their lives. Speculation, rejoicing, and attempts to retell the events to each other and to others
would consume their thoughts for the rest of their lives.

The fellowship of believers became the witnessing church that day.
Some years before, the idea had been planted, at Caesarea-Philippi
(Matt. 16:18-19). Its time had been in the hands of God. No clock
or calendar could predict it. In God's own time the Spirit came and
said in effect: "My children, this is the hour of the church—your hour.
You have been prepared for this. You have all you need to seize
this unique opportunity. Make haste now. Buy up your time carefully."
And to their everlasting credit, those folks reached out and grabbed
their moment and made the most of it for God, in honor of their
Lord and for the benefit of all mankind.

Let's not lose the grandeur of the moment, the monumental turn
that history made that day, by squabbling over the exact description
of the signs of the Spirit. There was a sound like a mighty rush of
wind. Wind is a timeless symbol of the Holy Spirit. Time and again
in the Old Testament the Spirit manifested himself as a wind (Gen.

8:1; Ex. 14:21; Ezek. 37:9-14). And the wind was powerful because the Holy Spirit is powerful.

Tonguelike wisps of fire rested over each of those present (v. 3). Fire signifies the presence of God. Purifying, cleansing, warmth-giving, dark-dispelling fire came and danced over each head. The presence of God was not for the apostles alone but for all who were present. God's gifts, his call, his mandate came to all the disciples. Pentecost singled out the Christians from the rest of the world; but within the group, it was a marvelous experience of leveling and equalizing. Peter's fire-tongue was no bigger or smaller than that of the most timid of the young women exalting breathlessly in that place of places, where time stopped for a moment and then started running in a brand-new direction.

"They were all filled with the Holy Spirit" (v. 4). Various gifts from God were distributed to all the folks there that morning. And they all began to speak in other tongues.

What do the tongues mean? What was happening? How normative was the experience for the future of the church?

The coming of the Holy Spirit at Pentecost was not the first time the Holy Spirit came to man. Our doctrine of the Trinity teaches us that God has always been present and active, not only as the Father and Son but also as the Spirit. The uniqueness of Pentecost is the dimension of commissioning and affirming that it imparted to the disciples. Jesus had promised that the Spirit would come. They were supposed to wait to begin their responsibilities until after the Spirit came. While wind, fire, and unusual language may not be normative for all Christians in every generation, a deep and abiding existential experience with the Holy Spirit is desirable for all of us. Though we may not all have the same mental and spiritual equipment and thus express the indwellingness of the Spirit in the same way, as followers of Jesus we have the Spirit. Our deficiency is in failing to claim what is already ours—namely, the Spirit—and in not acting with power and determination.

Speaking with tongues, *glossolalia,* was not instituted at Pentecost. There are evidences of ecstatic language in other religions of the ancient world. Some have even said that the noises the priests of Baal made on Carmel during their battle with Elijah were a form of language beyond language.

Most of us have had experiences that superseded or transcended language, either moments of great joy or great sorrow. Nothing in human language can express the terrible agony one feels when he hears about the sudden and tragic death of someone he loves. By the same token, when joyous moments come, we resort to banal expressions and dance an unchoreographed jig in an attempt to translate what we are feeling at the moment.

There is nothing wrong with ecstatic speech. The problem with the manifestation has always come when those who speak in tongues or those who deny the validity of the practice try to impose their own experience on the other group. Reading 1 Corinthians 12 and 14 should help us acquire the perspective and balance we need to handle such a gift of the Spirit.

But Luke refers to the speech in this passage as "other dialects" so that the hearers heard the message in language they recognized.

Because Pentecost was a major feast, Jews from all over the Roman world had gathered in their ancient and beloved city for the festival (v. 5). (Historical footnote: Because of the various persecutions, invasions, and subsequent deportations over a five- or six-century period of time, Jews were scattered throughout the Roman Empire. In addition to the forced dispersion, trade and economics served to scatter the Jews to other parts of the world. Then as now, however, through a fiercely maintained combination of religion and family, the Jews maintained their identity.)

Let's remind ourselves that God was selecting his own time for another part of his plan to be revealed. What better time to formally, undeniably introduce a faith designed to embrace all men everywhere than during a festival when the faithful from the corners of the earth were gathered! Later these faithful believers will share the gospel past the boundaries of Jerusalem and Palestine to the outer reaches of known civilization.

By reading between the lines in verses 6-11, we get the idea that the upper room quickly became too small to contain the zeal and excitement of the newly infused disciples. Rejoicing, laughing, and speaking jubilantly, they quickly spilled out into the streets. It would be quite natural for them to head for the spacious porches of the Temple, gathering crowds as they danced, praised, and rejoiced. At first handfuls, then dozens, and quickly hundreds and thousands flocked around to see and hear this new occurrence.

And amazingly enough, those cosmopolitian traders, teachers, scholars, merchants, minor government officials, and religious leaders from such exotic places as Parthia, Cappadocia, Egypt, Crete, and Arabia could understand what was going on. The ecstatic speech of the upper room, under the power of the Spirit, was translated into meaningful language.

Then in verses 12-13 appears the timeless reaction. Some looked at the people who were caught up in the phenomenon, heard the rejoicing in their own language, and blurted out, "What is happening? What does this mean for them, and what does it mean for me?" Others, probably more on the periphery of the crowd, scoffed, saying: "These people have had too much partying." An honest inquiry will likely lead one to the truth, but defenses quickly settle in place lest the unfamiliar infringe upon the familiar.

Peter's Sermon (2:14-40)

Speeches in Acts are an important vehicle for conveying the gospel, especially in Luke's wanting to set forth in an orderly manner what he considered a strategic theological statement. Since there were no scribes present to take down the messages verbatim, the presentations became a part of the remembered body of truth that was passed from person to person and church to church. Then Luke, under the leadership of the Holy Spirit, set down both what was said and what was remembered as having been said. He structured it all to set forth his particular points.

Peter delivered the first Christian apology (defense) in the history of the church (v. 14). In that first day of the church's life, Peter was not as concerned with setting forth a highly reasoned theological proposition as he was with making a defense for Christ as the promised Messiah. His sermon reflects a very basic, pre-Pauline theology. So basic and uncolored by later preaching and teaching was his message that most scholars accept the speech as essentially coming from the mouth of Peter on that day. It is not difficult to imagine that the sermon would have been indelibly stamped on the minds of many who heard it because of its incredible setting.

When Luke started writing, he had but to talk with a few of the living eyewitnesses of Pentecost and/or converse with some of the ones who were in the street as the sermon was delivered. By the time Luke wrote, Peter was probably dead; but Luke would have had several opportunities to talk with Peter to get the facts from the man himself. So, even if a bit of editing has taken place, we are hearing brilliant echoes from the day of Pentecost itself.

Several scholars describe many of the speeches in Acts, especially Peter's on Pentecost, as apostolic preaching. Even though the Old Testament proof texts vary from preacher to preacher and sermon to sermon, at least four common elements run through all the apostolic sermons: (1) an announcement that the Day of the Lord, long foretold, had at last dawned; (2) a restatement of the basic facts in the life of Jesus (birth, ministry, death, and resurrection); (3) the lifting of Old Testament Scriptures that prove the authenticity of Jesus as Messiah; (4) a call to decision, to repentance. As we read Peter's sermon, we can see these aspects of the message.

In verses 15-21 Peter cited the prophet Joel (2:28-32) as his authority for insisting that the Day of the Lord had indeed dawned. From the foundations of the old and the long promised, the new day is heralded.

Peter reiterated in verses 22-36 that Jesus, the man from Nazareth, is the Messiah. God affirms his messiahship by doing mighty works through him. The Jewish leaders would not accept Jesus as the sent one, so they killed him; but God miraculously raised him from the dead. Quoting a Davidic psalm (16:8-11), Peter insisted that King David foretold Jesus as the crucified but resurrected Messiah. The preacher went even further, shocking some of the listeners by saying that as great a king as David was, Jesus is superior. Then the final peroration to the sermon came when Peter declared: "Let all the house of Israel therefore know assuredly that God has made him both Lord and Christ, this Jesus whom you crucified" (v. 36).

Put yourself back on that Jerusalem street that bright morning. Hardly nine o'clock. People had just begun to stir when a great tumult broke out in the vicinity of Herod's Temple. News of a commotion telegraphed through the narrow streets of that ancient city and crowds. The people were always hungry for excitement and gathered from all parts of the city. Perhaps we can identify with their shock at Peter's announcement that a man named Jesus, from Nazareth no less, was the long-promised Messiah, the fulfillment of all their centuries of hopes, and the man upon whom they were supposed to pin their dreams. But he had been *crucified*. Unbelief. Incredulity. Anger. These and more emotions flooded through the throngs. No wonder so many of the Jews simply turned and walked away.

"What shall we do?" (v. 37). Peter's searing charge of their crucifixion of the Messiah cut hundreds in the hushed crowd to the heart. Sensitive, hungry souls they were. Willing to be open to the Holy Spirit, they could respond from the depths of their beings to the message that Peter delivered. Their desperate question was the beginning point of saving faith for them. Discipleship lay just beyond that question desperately hanging in the morning air.

Without hesitation the outspoken Peter gave his answer: "Repent, and be baptized" (v. 38). From the days of John the Baptist, Peter had been taught the necessity of repentance. Since the kingdom of God is a spiritual reality, only those born of the Spirit through a complete change of life (repentance) can live in the kingdom. Baptism became the outward symbol of the inward change that had taken place. The inward and outward would forever be linked as being the gateway into salvation and discipleship.

Peter, however, expanded on these two simple themes (vv. 38-40). Repentance and baptism are to be done in the name of Jesus Christ. He was not making a full-orbed Christological statement so much as he was uttering an invocation, a prayer that Jesus Christ would become part and parcel of their lives as a result of their repentance and baptism. Feel with Peter the intensity of the statement: Jesus Christ alone can give new life as a result of repentance and subsequent baptism.

Is baptism necessary for salvation and the remission of sins? There are Christian groups who vehemently insist that such is the case. Ignoring the inwardness of the Christian experience, forgetting Jesus' emphasis on the change of heart and attitude that is basic, they lift this verse and build a theological system on it. It is a violation of the tone and intent of the Christian faith to insist that the outward act has any value except as it is completed by true repentance within. Linked with repentance, baptism is an experience of confirmation and affirmation by the Holy Spirit.

The Flavor of the First New Community (2:41-47)

There is a direct connection between receiving the Word and acting on it. Those who received Peter's word acted on what they heard (vv. 41-42). They were baptized. This was a difficult step for many of them. Baptism had been reserved for Gentiles who converted to Judaism. The idea of having to be baptized would be repugnant to those born as Jews. Yet so deep was their conviction that the new had indeed come that they eagerly submitted to the rite. Three thousand were added to the church in one day. The new church was indeed well launched.

Repentance and baptism created a community. The new converts joyfully spent much time together studying the apostles' teaching. Who were those ordinary men to do the teaching? They had no theological degrees to display on their walls. These men had spent their young years studying the Scripture in synagogue schools. They did their graduate work under Jesus himself. The experiences of the resurrection, ascension, and Pentecost served as powerful catalysts for recall. The apostles were qualified to teach the new converts.

Real fellowship, always a hallmark of the church, expressed itself in two ways: breaking of bread and prayers. Though the theology of the Lord's Supper was far from formed, there is little doubt that this community from the first days of its existence remembered the Lord's sacrifice through the reenactment of the Last Supper. While many churches exercise an exclusive protection of the Lord's Supper, others let individual worshipers make their own decision whether to participate. Each person can submit to the judgment of God as to his or her own worthiness for communion.

The new community was further flavored by a healthy fear. Why not? Indications are that all manner of marvelous deeds were done in their midst.

A contagious commonality sprang up among them. They sold what they had and shared everything together. Through the centuries we who cling to things too much have tried to put that communalism in "perspective." We probably have missed some great adventures in living while unnecessarily weighing ourselves down with a frantic pursuit of things. History does have its examples of communities that have lived selflessly with varying degrees of success, but most of us remain suspicious of such extreme expressions of church. One spin-off of that primitive practice has been an endless series of grand philanthropic acts. If we have been unwilling to sell all, we have at least been willing to sell some for the benefits of others. We can admit that we have not gone far enough, but the world is infinitely better off because of the distance we have gone.

A summary of the flavor of the first weeks of the church is given in verse 46: They frequented the Temple (they had no other place of worship to which they could go; nor would it have occurred to them to find another place); they joyfully fellowshipped together in an attitude of praise and celebration. And for those first few months, before the radical nature of the demands of the new community began to emerge, the church found favor with all the people. Every day enthusiastic followers were added to their number.

Never again would life be so blissful for the church. They were honestly fulfilling the best of who they perceived themselves to be, and their world was enthusiastic. As time moved along, however, their popularity dramatically and painfully waned. Acceptance gave way to suspicion, which in turn gave way to ostracism and overt persecution.

Venturing Out (3:1-26)

Surprise upon surprise in the early months of the church is joined by an attitude of pushing through barriers, exploring the new, sailing with fresh winds. Anytime we open ourselves to the breath of the Spirit, we are in for surprises and are pushed to new frontiers.

Peter and his friends surely did not know much about what was happening to them. Every day held new adventure. But two things they did understand: All that was happening was from God; and they would sail in convoy with those new winds.

The First Recorded Healing (3:1-10)

On their way to the Temple one afternoon (vv. 1-2) Peter and John saw a man lame from birth who was begging for alms. It is not too farfetched to suggest that Peter and John had often passed the man as he lay in that same spot. Such a sight would not be at all uncommon. The infirm were drawn to the Temple, hoping, no doubt, that the attitude of worship would express itself in generosity.

But something was different this day. Peter and John really saw the fellow and felt some kind of rapport with him. Perhaps their lives were now so full of hope and excitement that they were moved by the utter hopelessness of the crippled man. Maybe one of the men suddenly recalled the words of Jesus when he urged, "If you have eyes to see, then see!" And they saw.

Peter and John offered healing in the name of Jesus Christ of Nazareth (vv. 3-10). Taking the outcast by the hand, Peter helped the
fellow onto his feet. After a moment of unsteadiness, the Scripture
says, strength came; and within an instant the man was walking and
leaping. Peter had his ego under control. He was not healing in his
own name. Jesus Christ was the source and power of the healing.
The healed cripple went into the Temple with his two benefactors,
walking and leaping and praising God every step of the way.

Naturally, such a commotion in the sacred confines of the Temple
would cause people to stop and take notice. When they recognized
the hysterical fellow running and leaping as the cripple who for years
had begged alms at the gate, they were amazed.

Peter, by now a seasoned preacher, took the occasion to give another
of his speeches, although he had not healed the man in order to
attract a crowd. He reached out to the man for the sake of the man;
but when the additional opportunity presented itself, he was bold
and quick to seize the advantage of the moment.

The Sermon in the Temple (3:11-26)

This sermon is another example of apostolic preaching. A compari-
son of this message with the one he preached at Pentecost will show
that Peter was increasing in eloquence as a preacher and was also
experiencing a deepening of his theology. But all in all it follows
the same pattern as his first address.

In verses 11-13 Peter gave the Old Testament foundations for his
assertions about Jesus as the Savior. The man from Nazareth fulfills
the Old Testament prophecies.

In jabbing language (vv. 14-16) Peter accused the entire company
assembled of being responsible for and guilty of the death of Jesus.
He charged that they killed the "Author of life," but God raised him
up. It was in the name of the living Jesus that the healing was offered,
accepted, and accomplished.

Peter urged the crowd (vv. 17-24) to repent so that their sins could
be erased and "that times of refreshing may come from the presence
of the Lord" (v. 19).

In verses 25-26 came the clincher: In Jesus the Jews realize their
destiny as sons of the covenant. Jesus was the fulfillment of all the
messianic promises and hopes of Hebrew history. Following after him
would lead the Jews into a relationship that would indeed internalize

and give reality to the spirit of the law. Jesus would facilitate the genuine covenant fellowship that God had wanted with his people all along. To follow after Jesus would not force one out of his ancient religion but would lead him into a fuller understanding of his heritage.

The ultimate break between Judaism and Christianity was not a historical or theological necessity. The Christian faith grew out of its Hebrew roots but did not have to depart from them. The Jews' hardness of heart forced the final and painful break. Peter was speaking the truth when he urged them to accept Jesus as the one who could make them fully Jewish, but the time was rapidly approaching when fewer and fewer of his Hebrew brothers would hear the message.

Storm Clouds Gather (4:1 to 5:42)

The easy time the church was enjoying could not last. It was inevitable, given the closedmindedness of the Jews in general and the leaders' determination to maintain control of the power center, that trouble would come. As the apostles and their followers gained notoriety, the already anxious leaders would begin to get terribly uneasy. God was good to give his new community a few months to get their bearings, but times of severe testing and still newer frontiers lay just around the corner.

The First Arrest (4:1-31)

The rulers of the Jews may have seen themselves as keepers of the uneasy peace among the Jews (vv. 1-3). They bore with equanimity the burden of leadership, or so they said. Actually they were grasping for power and were determined to keep their place at all costs. Thus when word came to them that two Christians had effected a healing and were preaching strange and hostile sermons, orders were issued to arrest the troublemakers. Since it was late in the afternoon, Peter and John were locked up until morning.

Hundreds of those who heard the sermon in the Temple became believers in Jesus (v. 4). Their lives were turned over to the Lord, who began his marvelous work of salvation. But the rulers overlooked the jubilation of the new believers, so consumed were they with keeping their own place of authority.

Talk about a surprise! Peter and John were in jail. They never bargained for prison. "John," Peter may have said, "what went wrong?
We were not bothering anyone. In fact, we were conduits of healing
to a lifelong cripple; and here we are in the dungeon!"

They were scared, embarrassed, and angry, all rolled up into one
heavy emotion. They had been around when Jesus clashed with these
same men, but it was an altogether new experience to be the brunt
of bureaucratic ire themselves.

But God was good to give them a night to get themselves together.
If they had been thrust immediately into the presence of the court,
they might not have claimed their inner resources to make the spirited
defense they did when they were called before the tribunal the next
day.

When morning came, the two common men were led before the
august rulers and religious leaders of the land (vv. 5-12). Luke listed
all the important people who gathered to hear Peter and John. Ordi-
narily the court would have made short and largely unnoticed shrift
of two Galilean troublemakers. But these two were followers of Jesus,
in whose condemnation proceedings many of those present would
have participated. These shakers and movers had discounted rumors
that Jesus came back to life, choosing rather to believe that they
had rid the land of a potential threat to law and order (and to their
own power). But here were followers of Jesus back in the limelight.
At any rate, when word of the upcoming hearing got out through
the Sanhedrin grapevine, apparently an unusual number of officials
came to watch and, if necessary, render a judgment.

With scorn the questioner demanded of the two disciples, "By what
power have the likes of you been able to do this healing?"

The world has never understood the power of the church. The
world has never understood the power of even a handful of devoted
followers of Christ. (Unfortunately, most of the time the church itself
has failed to recognize its inherent power.)

It is hard to say what kind of answer the rulers expected, but what
they got caught them completely off guard. The disciples may have
looked like unsophisticated men from Galilee. But Peter surprised
them by giving a disturbingly effective defense. (The night with the
Lord had been just the time of energizing that he needed.)

The rulers wanted to know by what power the crippled man had
been enabled to walk. Their answer was by the power of Jesus of

Nazareth, whom they had so recently condemned to die. But God would not let him stay dead and had raised him from the dead. This same risen Christ was the source of power. Recalling for them Psalm 118:22, one of their famous messianic testimonies, Peter insisted that Jesus, the stone they had rejected as of no consequence, had become the cornerstone. And to add insult to injury, the bold Peter exclaimed, "There is salvation in no other than this Jesus. By him alone does salvation come to a person or to a nation."

The Sanhedrin correctly assessed that Peter and John had not only kept company with Jesus but had appropriated the spirit of the man (v. 13). These same leaders would remember the unperturbable calm with which Jesus had faced those predawn hours when he was dragged before the court for judgment. They knew that Jesus knew he was facing death; and while he certainly did not welcome the prospect, neither did he cringe in fear. The two men who now stood before the Sanhedrin, easily, eloquently defending themselves, had that same maddening quality of calm. How could leaders manage a people without fear as the tool? Whence came the sure logic and easy flow of language that Peter used to state his case? That too must have something to do with his relationship with Jesus.

Mirrors of Jesus, that's what these men were. A shudder ran over some of the judges because they surely did not want to get into the Jesus issue again. They had settled his case and did not want to reopen it.

Tempted as they might have been to quietly dispatch Peter and John to the lowest part of the dungeon or to secretly order their deaths, the rulers restrained themselves (vv. 14-18). After all, there stood the healed man. The crowd, though manageable, would put up a howl if anything drastic were done to the new healers. In their consternation the judges sent the two disciples out of the courtroom so that they could decide what to do with them. In their "wisdom" they decided to do nothing, at least at this point, except reprimand the men and give them a stern warning not to preach in Jesus' name again.

Peter and John made a very difficult choice (vv. 19-22) when they fearlessly, if somewhat cautiously, retorted to the judges, "Your honors, we realize the risk we are taking; but we are compelled to keep on speaking and preaching what we have felt, seen, and heard."

Visibly shaken by Peter's quiet but firm retort, the elders shook their long, bony fingers in the disciples' faces, threatened them further, and let them go.

As soon as they were released, the two disciples beat a hasty retreat to the place where their friends were gathered, no doubt fervently in prayer for the safety of Peter and John (vv. 23-31). It must have been a sobering moment for the entire community. They had enjoyed such warm acceptance by the populace. Did this arrest signal a new turn in their ministry? Many among them likely sensed that more of that kind of danger lay ahead for the group. The authorities would not long tolerate any real or imagined threat to their security; and they would not hesitate to use force if necessary to thwart any challenge.

How wonderful it is to have friends to whom we can flee when life becomes difficult. Before the Sanhedrin the young men were brave and sure; but, as always, there was an aftershock when confidence wavered and the future was not quite as rosy as it had appeared just the day before. In the fellowship of the church they found the wellsprings of fresh spiritual water to revive their spirits. With a community like theirs to offer mutual support, no threat of the Sanhedrin could ultimately intimidate.

The group rejoiced over the courageous way that Peter and John had conducted themselves and celebrated the worthy witness they had given to the Lord Jesus. Quoting from Psalm 2, the group took the occasion of the deliverance as a chance to worship and honor God. While they prayed, the place was shaken; and they were all filled with the Holy Spirit and felt emboldened in their souls.

More of the Common Life (4:32-37)

The closing verses of this chapter give us more clues as to the nature of the common life. As people came into the community, they committed themselves completely to the cause of Jesus, even to the point of selling what they owned and making the gain available to the church. One of those notable early followers was Barnabas, who was one of the major disciple/missionaries of the early church. He divested himself of all worldly entanglements so that he could be completely free to move about as the Spirit directed him.

Ananias and Sapphira (5:1-11)

This episode lays to rest any notion that Acts is a stylized glossy picture of a primitive church blissfully at peace with itself. The Bible never slides over the sins of its characters, showing rather, in all honesty, their shortcomings and failures.

The story is familiar (vv. 1-2). A man and his wife became participants in the new community. No doubt they were glad to be a part of the movement and were serious about their involvement. But then Barnabas and some of the others began to divest themselves of their goods and give all to the church. Admiring members of the fellowship applauded such selfless acts. Ananias and Sapphira were not as secure as Barnabas. Whereas Barnabas could freely and with no strings attached give his money to the church and brush aside the flattery, Ananias and his wife craved the adulation but could not quite bring themselves to part with all their goods. They would go after the best of both worlds: sell the property and make a show of giving it to the church, but keep part of the proceeds hidden "just in case of a rainy day."

The sin lay not in keeping part of the proceeds but in lying about the entire matter. The phrase "kept back" is like our term embezzlement. The man embezzled from God.

Peter saw through the attempt (vv. 3-4). How? Maybe the look in the man's eyes. Maybe suspicious talk. No matter. Peter was no mind reader, but he did grasp the situation.

"Ananias, you have falsified God's Spirit within you." The language is stronger than "lying to the Spirit." The fellow had violated his own integrity, perjured the very Spirit of God who now lived in his life, and made a mockery of the Holy Spirit's activity in his soul. Something far more devastating than a common lie had erupted in Ananias' life: The glorious work of grace begun in and for Ananias was counted for nothing.

Beyond the personal implications of his act, Ananias had brought shame and reproach to the church. Veteran disciples were grieved, new converts were given a stumbling block, and the world was given fuel for scoffing.

The enormity of his sin came crashing in on the hapless fellow (vv. 5-6). His most honest moment was also his last, as he realized for the first time the folly of playing games with himself, with his community, and most of all with God.

Why did he die? Did God reach down and instantly condemn him to death for his sin? Was he killed by the Lord as an example for others who would falsify the Spirit in their own lives? In that blinding moment of honesty and clarity, was Ananias so ashamed that his heart literally broke? Was his terror at the range of possibilities of punishment so great that life was shocked out of his body? No one knows the answer, but the account is too vivid to deny the man's death. Ananias was joined in death within a few hours by his wife.

Such immediate and radical judgment is not the usual way God deals with us. Judgment is more often tempered with mercy. We trust Christ for salvation, so we do not have to go around looking over our shoulders lest God reach down and snuff out our lives like one would a pesky moth around a light bulb.

However, judgment, punishment for sin, and retribution are parts of God's way of running a balanced moral universe. We need to get the message that we do not go on sinning with impunity, thinking that we are above having to reckon with God and others for our misdeeds.

Whatever the reasons, Ananias fell dead; and the young men wrapped him in graveclothes and buried him. They did not even take the time to notify Sapphira. It was common practice to bury the deceased on the same day, since embalming was not practiced, but such haste was unusual. Maybe those who witnessed the death had enough superstition to want to get rid of the body as quickly as possible.

Three hours later Sapphira came in (vv. 7-10). Maybe Peter had sent for her. When the apostle confronted her with their joint sin, she too fell dead; and the same pallbearers prepared her body for burial and placed her beside her husband.

Great fear came upon the church (v. 11). All the events of recent months were enough to make any group uneasy. Pentecost. Healings. Bucking the authorities. And now these two incredible deaths. Fear, a healthy respect for the power of God, and the dynamism of the new community tended to further season the believers in their new relationships with God through Christ. Great issues, even eternal issues, were at stake here. These men and women were not involved in a passing fad, a religious lark; God was working, and they were part of his work.

A footnote: The word for church, *ekklesia*, is first used in Acts in 5:11. The English word *church* translated the Greek word *ekklesia*, which meant a free assembly of people. The Christian *ekklesia* was old and new: new in that it gave testimony to the life, death, resurrection, and ongoing ministry of Jesus; and old because the idea of the assembly reached back to the Hebrew synagogue gathering. We should be grateful for the new and the old in our Christian experience.

Mixed Response to Ministry (5:12-16)

The apostles were admired, but from a safe distance (vv. 12-13). No doubt these were men from God, but they were rather rapidly becoming a thorn in the Establishment's side. So the throng was increasingly skeptical and hesitant to openly identify with the new movement.

But growth occurred in spite of caution (vv. 14-16). In those heyday times of the church, Peter and the other apostles could facilitate divine healing. Such an aura grew up around the indefatigable Peter that his shadow was regarded as therapeutic. Some laid their infirm loved ones along the street, hoping that the apostle's shadow would fall across the person and cause healing. We should note that the Scripture does not say that Peter's shadow ever healed anyone—only that folks thought such a thing might take place.

In Jail Again—This Time with Company (5:17-42)

Aggravation at the apostles' preaching quickly turned to anger as the momentum of the new movement visibly picked up steam (vv. 17-21a). Every day reports of healing, miracles, and increasing numbers of converts reached the halls of the Sanhedrin, causing a rising crescendo of noisy concern among the elders. Finally the situation became so intolerable in the eyes of the leaders that the high priest and the Sadducees ordered a mass arrest of all twelve of the apostles. Probably moving very quickly lest they stir up the population, Temple police rounded up the apostles and clapped them in a common jail—one single cell.

Peter and John had been there before, but this was a first for most, if not all, the other apostles. Christ's cup was being passed from mouth to mouth, and all were drinking deeply of the bitter dregs. Since they were "veteran" prisoners, Peter and John may have spent some time encouraging their brothers, assuring them of the Lord's presence. "Deliverance will come," Peter promised. Little did he know that deliverance would come in such a dramatic manner.

Luke wrote, on the authority of careful research and as much person-to-person conversation as he could manage, that during the night an angel came, opened the prison doors, and told them to take up their preaching stations in the Temple at dawn's first light. *The New English Bible* says, "Tell them about this new life and all it means." What a glorious charge to preach a whole gospel so that man's life can be completed in Christ!

In all their pomp and circumstance, the high priest and his crowd assembled in the judgment hall and regally summoned the prisoners (vv. 21*b*-32). Pity the poor courier who had to come back, hat in hand, with head bowed low, to say, "Your lordship, they are gone. The doors are closed. The guards are on duty. Nothing in the cell is disturbed, but the men are gone." Rage! Hysteria! Off-with-your heads fulminations reverberated in that impressive chamber. But the fact remained: The apostles of Jesus were gone.

Just then a messenger came puffing into the room and loudly declared, "They are in the Temple preaching. The men we put in jail yesterday afternoon are in the Temple this morning, saying the same things they were saying when we arrested them."

No fool, that wily old high priest. "Go, bring them to us; but do them no harm, stir no violence," he said, obviously struggling for control.

This time the apostles were not hassled. They were invited to appear before the Sanhedrin to discuss the issues at hand.

"Why do you persist?" entreated the high priest in subdued but seething tones. "We plainly told you not to preach in that name anymore."

If there had been hesitation before when Peter declared that he simply had to preach the gospel, there was certainly none now. All the apostles assembled before the court were in full agreement: "We must obey God rather than men" (v. 29). His words implied: "So there! We've said it, and we are glad; and what's more, we are prepared to take anything you can mete out. We have discovered brand-new meaning in our lives that makes suffering bearable."

And as if he were rubbing salt into open wounds, Peter stated fearlessly, "God sent Jesus as the Messiah, but you hanged him on a tree; you crucified him. We are witnesses to the redemption that comes from repentance and acceptance of him as Lord of life."

The elders nearly lost all control (vv. 33-39). Never ones to dirty their hands with executions, preferring to have such nasty deeds done by others, they were so angry at the apostles for their boldness and for their impertinence that they almost rushed out of their seats to slay the peasants right there on the spot.

The famous Gamaliel saved the day. In the midst of the shouting and gesturing and wild threats, he rose to speak. "Men of Israel. Let's calm down and think this thing through. Sure, these unlearned men are irritating. But they may well be from God. Let's leave them alone. If their movement is empty, it will die of its own anemia. If it is from God (did he secretly believe, hope that it was?) and we fight it, we will be in the terribly dangerous position of fighting against God himself."

Not willing to take on the people if executions had been ordered, the Sanhedrin ordered the apostles to never preach again. To add emphasis to the sentence, the men were soundly beaten (vv. 40-42). The beating did just about as much good as beatings usually do— none. In fact, the apostles rejoiced that they had been allowed to suffer for their Lord. Their backs hurt on the outside, but their heart exulted on the inside.

The apostles did not quit preaching. Every day in the Temple and at home they ceaselessly preached Christ.

Under Fire the Church Expands
6:1 to 9:31

Getting Organized (6:1-7)

Organization in the church grew out of the life of the congregation. As the days went by and Jesus did not return for his flock, and as more and more people became believers, some semblance of structure and organization became a necessity. One looks long and hard in Jesus' teachings for a plan of organization. He left such details to the good sense of the church people, as they reflected on their needs and were sensitive to the leadership of the Holy Spirit.

Two things stand out in the process of these early attempts at organization: (1) The apostles, especially Peter, took a leading role in shaping organization, but (2) the congregation was always integrally involved. Simon, exercising his innate leadership abilities, led the church in making decisions and choices. But any way one reads the account of the earliest churches, he comes away with a definite impression of participatory government.

Most churches echo those basic soundings. While on the one hand they look for and respond to pastoral leadership, on the other hand they insist on congregational participation. There is no room in the New Testament church for a monarchial ruler, but neither does a congregation ever outgrow its need for some form of pastoral guidance.

Growing Pains (6:1)

It is difficult to determine just how much time elapsed between chapter 5 and chapter 6, but the days were fruitful. Luke began this important transitional chapter by stating (v. 1) that the followers of Jesus were increasing steadily in number.

The Lord tarried his coming; and every day dozens, even hundreds, of people in Jerusalem professed belief in Jesus as the Messiah, received baptism, and became part of the burgeoning congregation. This growth and change was almost too much for the twelve and probably others of that initial "upper-room" crowd.

People not of Jewish background were seeking membership. Jews from other parts of the world who happened to be in town on business or pilgrimages were caught up in the contagion of the gospel, asked probing questions, and made significant commitments of life to the Lord Jesus. None of the Gentiles yet many of the Jews of the dispersion were orthodox in their religious practices. The inner circle had been reared as strict Jews but had not yet heard with their hearts' ears the universality of the gospel. Frankly, they were having a terrible time coping with all these new people and their varied religious perspectives. Yes, growth presented its share of problems. Surprise and chagrin were the overriding emotions.

The Hellenists about whom Luke spoke were people of Jewish descent who had been moved or scattered to far-flung reaches of the Roman Empire over many decades. Though many retained the liturgical Hebrew, and maybe even some Aramaic, Greek was their major language. With the Greek language came certain Greek ways of thinking. These Greek-speaking Jews, Hellenists (Hellene is another word for Greece), remained basically true to the faith of their fathers. But living in the Roman Empire, rubbing shoulders with people of every nationality and philosophy, they naturally moved toward more openness in regard to different races and religions.

By contrast, the men and women who had always been in Palestine, in or around Jerusalem and Galilee, obviously had a much narrower world view. As is often the case, the "home folks" were not a little suspicious of their "city cousins" from Rome, Philippi, Alexandria, Antioch, and other places in Caesar's world. Since tension between these two mind-sets existed throughout Palestine, it is no wonder that friction erupted within the church.

There is no evidence that the needy among the Hellenistic Christians were actually being neglected by the Hebrew Christians; but when such problems exist in the minds of the people, they must be dealt with.

Help from the Congregation (6:2-7)

When the problem came out in the open, the apostles summoned the congregation and pleaded for help (v. 2). In their own minds at least, the twelve were spending an inordinate amount of time dealing with the thorny problems of who got fed, how much, and when.

Both to free themselves from such a ticklish situation and to give them more time for prayer, study, and preaching, they asked for and got help from the congregation.

Beware of making this episode too foundational in the ministry because there are implicit dangers that erupt if this experience is made into a hard and fast principle. The pastor of the church cannot divest himself from administration. Most churches and pastors who get in trouble do so at the point of poor administration. The management of the church is either too much in the hands of the pastor or too much in the hands of the "board" of deacons; or the pastor cannot or refuses to exercise the givenness of his role as a leader. So the congregation falls upon itself and begins to fight and squabble.

As ideal as it sounds for the pastor to leave "waiting of tables" to the deacons, such is most often not the case; nor is it completely desirable. The genius of administration in a church is that of shared responsibility. As pastor and people learn to trust each other, and as they discover their several gifts, the day-by-day management of the institution can be borne by a number of people, thus freeing the pastor to more completely focus on the primary responsibilities of his ministry.

All believers are called to be ministers, or servants. A further reading in Acts will reveal that these seven who were elected may have done some waiting on tables, but they were far beyond that initial job description. Philip and Stephen became effective preachers and witnesses for Christ. Popular tradition has all of the seven actively involved in ministry, some finally dying a martyr's death for their faith. Pastors and lay leaders cheat themselves when either party is content to let the laity take care of details while the pastor does the so-called important things like preaching, visiting, and general ministering. The pivotal doctrine of the priesthood of believers demands that each be about his own calling. The expression of calling must not be limited to the spiritual for the preacher and the secular for the laymen. If a Christian layman can run a multimillion-dollar bank or corporation, he can surely take a larger hand in the total life of the church than simply serving on the finance committee. Sad to say, clergy and laymen often do not know what to do with each other. There might be less rivalry if ministers and lay people were more actively involved in full-fledged ministry.

"[You] pick out . . . seven men of good repute, full of the Spirit and of wisdom, whom *we* may appoint" (v. 3). Democracy in action. The congregation was charged with the responsibility of at least nominating the seven. Perhaps the apostles' role was ratification of the congregation's choices.

Seven *men.* Many churches are in the throes of deciding about ordination of women to be deacons and ministers in the church. In ever-increasing numbers, Protestant churches are ordaining women to serve the church. There is no doubt but that Luke has the church naming seven *men.* Paul described the office of deacon in his pastoral letters in terms of maleness. But we must balance the maleness of these specific statements with other grand principles such as neither male nor female; Jew nor Greek; slave nor free; and so on. Paul called Phoebe a deaconess in Romans 16:1. Each church must decide its own practice here, but each should leave room for varying opinions.

As rapidly as the church was growing, the apostles needed all the prayer and study time they could get (v. 4). No doubt the new deacons did free up the apostles' time.

Seven men were elected as deacons (vv. 5-6). All seven have Greek names, suggesting that they were all Hellenistic Jews from various parts of the empire.

Practically nothing is known of the seven. Stephen, the first Christian martyr, is listed first. Philip and Stephen quickly left the tables and became preachers of ability and renown. Extrabiblical tradition has Prochorus becoming secretary to John the Beloved, the writer of Revelation and the books bearing his name, and finally suffering martyrdom in Antioch of Syria. Nicolaus was not even a native-born Jew but was a proselyte, a convert to Judaism.

The number seven is one of the divine numbers of perfection (seven days, seven lampstands, seven visions, etc.). The fact that the first church had only seven deacons does not limit future Christian churches to seven deacons.

There is debate concerning the link between the seven in early Acts and the subsequent development of a full office of deacon in later years, but there is no doubt that the office of deacon had its genesis in those first days of the Jerusalem church. The standards set for these first seven continue to stand us in good stead as we seek lay leaders in our contemporary churches.

Who did the ordaining; who laid on hands? Only the twelve? or the entire congregation? That is not clear either. The local church or a specific denomination has to make those decisions.

Perhaps as a result of the multiplication of ministry made possible by the election and commissioning of the seven, the work of the Lord expanded even more dramatically in the next months (v. 7). As the preaching increased, so did the number of converts. Even priests were saved and became followers of Jesus. 'Twas a great day in the life of the Lord's church.

Stephen (6:8 to 7:60)

Biographical Sketch (6:8)

Commentators are generally agreed that had Stephen lived, he would have gone down in history as one of the all-time great Christian leaders. Every indication is that he was a brilliant thinker and preacher with marvelous gifts of the Holy Spirit. Even in his death he gives every Christian faith and courage for living and dying. No one could have met such a grisly death with greater calmness or assurance than did this young Hellenistic Jew.

Stephen was "full of grace and power" (v. 8). One of the shades of meaning of the word *charis*, from which the word grace is translated, is charm. Beneath our shallow idea of charm is a richer word that gives a clue about personality. Stephen was charming in that he was easy to be with, warm and personable, and willing to give himself to other people. But he was a man of power. Kindness, humility, and gentleness do not preclude strength, vigor, determination, and courage.

We get our word dynamite from the Greek word for power, *dunamis*. Stephen, Peter, and many other early Christians were people full of the "dynamite" of God. No wonder Jews and Romans alike, shaky in their own corroding places of power, feared these men and women who were obviously electrified by an unearthly force. Stephen had opened himself to the best of what God in Christ had to offer— fullness of grace and power.

God, working in him, performed signs and wonders among the people. Healing, demon exorcising, prophesying, effective preaching, and teaching flowed out of the life of this dedicated young believer.

Stephen's Mistake (6:9-10)

Stephen made a mistake, at least in the eyes of the natural Jews. When Jesus said to go to all nations and peoples, Stephen took him seriously and began to preach to Gentiles and to spend a considerable amount of time in synagogues made up of Hellenistic Jews. The orthodox Jews looked with prejudice and condescension on those "foreign" Jews. With his winsomeness, intellect, dedication, and Hellenistic background, Stephen apparently made great inroads with those Jews. Jealousy and suspicion flared among the Establishment, triggering acrimonious debate with Stephen.

Dirty Tricks (6:11-14)

The Jews could not bear Stephen's security in Christ, and they surely could not defeat him in debate; so they resorted to dirty tricks. They made up lies against him. Isn't it incredible that the Jews would stir up lies to defeat a fellow Jew in a religious debate!

The Establishment's trick in this instance was to quote what Stephen and the other Christians were saying, lift the statements out of context, and twist them to serve their own evil purposes. Jesus never said he would destroy the Temple, a place that he loved; but he did predict its destruction. Jesus insisted that he had come to fulfill the best of the Mosaic code, not to displace the laws of Moses. If the Jews had not become so afraid, they could have seen that Jesus' intention was to give continuity to the grand, noble Jewish tradition. Too bad the Jews could not separate the eternality of the Ten Commandments from traditions whose usefulness was set in a certain day but which could be supplanted or enhanced by later revelation.

On the basis of the lies, the ramrods of the opposition had Stephen hauled into court for a trial before the Sanhedrin. The Pharisees and scribes cast in their lots with their religious/political enemies, the Sadducees, to create a kangaroo court for Stephen. One look at the unsavory witnesses should have convinced the judges to throw Stephen's case out of court, but the leaders of the people were so anxious to get rid of this gentle but strong man that they prostituted their leadership.

Stephen's Speech (6:15 to 7:53)

When the accusers were finished hurling their scurrilous charges at the Christian leader, the high priest had already made up his mind about the verdict. But to maintain a semblance of proper procedure, he turned to the accused to see if he had anything to say for himself (v. 15). Spectators recalled later that as Stephen began to speak, his face had an inner glow and actually shone like that of an angel. In John 17:22 Jesus had promised his followers his own glory, his own glow from God. Stephen strikingly demonstrated that inner fire as he started to speak.

Using the literary device of a speech so popular in Acts, Luke drew from eyewitness sources to reconstruct Stephen's stirring address (vv. 1-8). Remember that this is a speech, not a closely reasoned theological position. Stephen evidently knew the Greek version of the existing Old Testament, the Septuagint, thoroughly, and was able to make easy but commanding use of that Scripture.

The point of the sermon is that God never bound himself to one land and certainly not to the Temple in Jerusalem. As a Hellenistic Jew, a man of the world, Stephen would emphasize the universality of the gospel, insisting that God had never intended for any of his revelation to be limited to the Jews alone. It was for this preachment, coupled with his "blasphemous" statement that he could see Jesus at the right hand of God, that he was executed.

Abraham was not a native of Palestine. In fact, strictly speaking, he was not a Jew but a man from Mesopotamia, whom God called out of his native land. Circumcision, a rite whose antecendents are not known and whose actual significance is not clear, was given a crucial place in Hebrew history. The pagan practice was sanctified as the outward sign of the inner covenant between God and his people.

The revered patriarchs, titular leaders of the twelve tribes, were anything but willing participants in the plan of God (vv. 9-16). They connived to have Joseph destroyed, lied to their father, and were generally rascals. Only by the providence of God did any good purpose come out of their wicked deeds. Stephen's point was not missed by his judges. God was moving again in a mighty way in the new community; but the rulers of Jerusalem, like the patriarchs of old, were showing a fierce unwillingness to cooperate. Another burr under the Establishment's saddle.

In a new and fresh rendition of the history of Moses, Stephen drove home the point that the Law Giver was first rejected by the Hebrews he was ordained by God to save (vv. 17-43). The slaves could not recognize in Moses their deliverer, ridiculing him rather than rallying behind his moral indignation at the condition of his people. When God sent Moses back to the people, they were forced to recognize his authority and commissioning from God. Once again, Stephen seemed to say, Jewish leaders are refusing to recognize God's deliverer. As God allowed the Hebrews to worship the golden calf in the wilderness for a season and later let them chase after other idols and the starry hosts, but severely judged their infidelity, so is he now prepared to judge his people if they reject this new revelation in Jesus. Quoting from Amos 5:25-27, Stephen held up the frightening prospect of more spiritual exile for the Jews if they turned their back on the fullness of the knowledge of God in Jesus.

God directed the building of the tabernacle in the wilderness and permitted the construction of the Temple in Jerusalem, but all along he made it perfectly clear that he would not be confined to a house made with hands (vv. 44-50). The revered patriarchs were pulled by God, kicking and screaming, into his plans. Their Hebrew ancestors had rejected Moses' leadership. Now God was threatening to turn his back once more on hardhearted Jews. There was no mistaking the rapier thrust of Stephen's speech.

His last lines were the final fuel tossed onto their smoldering tempers. "Stiff-necked, spiritually uncircumcised, Holy-Spirit-resisting people—you have always ridiculed the prophets and slain God's anointed deliverers. Now you have committed the supreme capital crime: You have murdered God's righteous one."

The Lynch Mob (7:54-60)

Too much. "You have gone too far!" The rumble in the crowd became a roar. Had the lynch mob been primed by some of the Jewish leaders? Was there a semblance of the pronouncement of a judgment? In the rush of those final moments, who can say accurately what actually happened? It is reasonably clear that even though Stephen had fired some slashing words to the rulers, he had committed no crime deserving death—no blasphemy had actually been uttered. Mob mentality is a frightening mania.

Religious movies have attempted to reconstruct the scene: rulers whose venal pride had been deeply wounded, a motley mob feigning indignation but actually just thirsty for some blood, with the calm young man, center stage in this melodrama, suddenly transfixed by a vision from God.

Swiftly, before Roman soldiers could be alerted, Stephen was dragged, kicked, and tossed outside the city gates, thrown into the stoning pit, and quickly bludgeoned to death by the jagged baseball- and basketball-sized stones. In his final gasps, pain was supplanted by God's gift of a vision. He died not in fear and despair but in victory and transcendence.

A while back—whether months or years we do not know—some of those same high- and low-class hooligans had stood at the foot of a cross and said, "That's the end of that." But it wasn't. They still had not learned the lesson that martyrs' blood simply enriches the ground from which springs even more martyrs. Stephen's death was certainly not the end of anything. Quite to the contrary, his death was another phase in the beginning of a new community that God was bringing into existence.

Providential Persecution (8:1-3)

Enter: Saul of Tarsus (8:1a)

It was no accident of fate, no simple quirk of destiny, that young Saul of Tarsus witnessed the death of Stephen. Even though the Scripture does not say so directly, it is not difficult to imagine that Saul's soul was already in turmoil. Who could hear the cogent reasonings of Stephen concerning the Christ, watch the resolute way in which he faced his accusers, and see the courageous way in which Stephen died without having his own spirit stirred? Like most of us when something really gets to us, Saul got frantically busy, attempting to shake off the experience. Unable or unwilling to admit his feelings, he vented all his fears and frustrations on the believers. With the fury of a summer storm, he burst on the church, determined to stamp out this insidious movement. But all he succeeded in doing was fur- thering and hastening the spread of the gospel.

The Gospel in Samaria (8:1b)

Fleeing from Jerusalem, new converts went to the outer regions of Judea and even into Samaria. Going into Samaria was another of those unplanned surprises made possible by necessity and the provi- dence of God. Orthodox Jews would have nothing to do with Samari- tans, whom they considered half-breeds racially and religiously. But when a near-mad persecutor is in hot pursuit, one would even take up with Samaritans if doing so meant refuge and safety. It is of lasting credit to the early converts that they pushed through their prejudices not only to live with the Samaritans, but to give them witness of the gospel. Later on we will see how effective the witness actually was.

One bit of information is slipped into verse 1: The apostles stayed in Jerusalem. Why? Perhaps because they were needed in the city. Perhaps the Hellenistic Jews consorting with Gentiles came under the heaviest attack. Some commentators say that the apostles were having a hard time adjusting to the idea of the universality of the gospel, of looking beyond the confines of Judaism to understand the broad scope of the gospel. Thus they would have remained in Jerusalem by choice. If this latter reason is the accurate one, subsequent extrabiblical accounts show these men catching the worldwide vision of the good news and penetrating the farthest reaches of the empire with their message. The glory of the gospel is that under its power, people can and do change.

Stephen Is Buried (8:2)

The regulations of the Jews permitted burial for a criminal who had been stoned to death but prohibited any lamentation over him. Stephen's friends, however, disobeyed the rules and buried him with much lamentation and mourning. He had been their friend, their leader, and a capable scholar. His death was a travesty of justice and likely caused a wave of uneasiness through the other church members for fear that they might be next to pay the supreme price for their faith.

The Lion of Judah (8:3)

Venting his anger, Saul went tearing through the city and its environs, ferreting out converts, disrupting worship services, and hauling men and women off to prison. Such "holy" crusades quickly lose all bounds of reason, all touch with reality; and Saul's vendetta was no different. Even though the language is sparse, the picture is a terrible one of midnight raids, good people poorly treated, and human rights disregarded in the name of religion—in the name of the God who created the world, described it as good, and sent his own Son to complete the process of redemption. Incredible!

Meet Philip (8:4-40)

Undaunted Preachers (8:4)

Ripped from their homes and families, probably having had their property confiscated, hounded out of town if they were lucky, and fleeing under cover of darkness if they were unlucky, followers of the Way ran from Jerusalem in every direction. But they remained undaunted, counting themselves blessed to be able to suffer persecution for their Lord. Everywhere they went, in their exodus from the Holy City, they preached. If there were any regrets over their decision to follow Christ, they quickly worked through them and eagerly shared the good news with all they met.

Philip Investigates (8:5-8)

Philip, one of the seven, was sent by the Spirit to a city of Samaria to preach. Going to Samaria, a place despised by orthodox Jews, would pose no problem for this Hellenized young Jew. Time and again Luke showed that these Jews who had been exposed to Greek culture were much more able to see the universal implications of the gospel than the Jews who had spent all their lives under the direct sway of Temple Judaism.

Philip's preaching was widely accepted, especially when he was able to perform signs and wonders in their midst, such as healing and exorcising unclean spirits. There was much joy in the city because so many infirm persons were restored to health and because large numbers responded to the gospel. (Later on we will see that belief on the basis of the miraculous is often shallow.)

Simon the Magician Believes (8:9-13)

The Oriental world has always been dotted with people who have apparent special powers. Simon Magus, Simon the Magician, evidently possessed something of these powers (vv. 9-11)—either the ability to operate mind over matter or the capacity to skillfully con people into believing in him as a man of super powers. Not only did he entertain with his magic; he was able to make the crowds believe that he could read minds and foretell the future.

When Philip came preaching, many of the Samaritans believed the gospel and were baptized (vv. 12-13). Even Simon turned to the new faith and was baptized.

Peter Investigates Samaria and Meets Simon (8:14-25)

Many Samaritans believed the gospel and came to faith in Jesus. Philip and the other Hellenistic Jews were not at all surprised, but those struggling orthodox Jewish men were having a difficult time believing that the Samaritans had become followers of the Way of Jesus. After all, despising Samaritans was almost a national tradition of the Jews. "Peter," they said, "You had better take a trip down there and investigate that situation. Strange. Yes, strange indeed. Go. Then come back and give us a full report" (author's paraphrase of v. 14).

When he got there, he found genuine believers in the Lord. But they had not received the Holy Spirit (vv. 15-17). He prayed for them and laid his hands on them. Then the Holy Spirit "fell" on the Samaritans just as it had fallen on the upper room at Pentecost. "That's right," he would later report. "They received the Spirit with the same manifestations that we did."

Why had the Holy Spirit not come before? Probably because no one had told them about the Spirit. No one had told the Samaritans about the possibility of the visitation of the Spirit, so they did not ask for the experience.

One important principle of evangelism is extraordinarily accurate: *People tend to be converted at the level of the group by which and into which they are converted.* The deeper the faith of the group into which a person is converted, the deeper will be his own faith as he enters that particular community. If the tone of a church is flippant about Christian conversion, those who join that fellowship will tend to reflect the flippant attitude. However, if we take seriously our Christian commitment and make that seriousness clear to new converts, they will tend to reflect our attitude.

No one had told the Samaritans about the Spirit. That dimension of Christian experience was missing from the group. But when Peter, who had experienced that dimension of experience, came and informed them of the grand possibility, they eagerly opened the windows of their souls to receive God's gift of the Holy Spirit.

Simon the Magician could not believe his eyes (vv. 18-24). When Peter prayed and laid his hands on people, they manifested the Holy

Spirit, probably by speaking in tongues. If only he could have that power, his act would really be a winner. Now his shallow commitment to Christ became abundantly evident. He saw the invoking of the Holy Spirit as a way to enhance his magic show, missing entirely the energizing experience of the coming of the Spirit into one's life. He had the temerity and stupidity to offer to buy the gift from Peter.

He had bargained with the wrong man. Peter told him in no uncertain terms what to do with his money. In biting language (reminiscent of his days as a fisherman), Peter informed the startled charlatan that he had never really had an experience with Jesus and that he would never receive the Holy Spirit in his present frame of mind and heart. "Repent. Ask for forgiveness. You are in the chains of sin and iniquity."

Simon was thunderstruck and terrified and begged Peter to send no evil hex on him. Some of those extrabiblical accounts say that Simon wept the entire time that Peter was verbally lashing him for his affront to God. Luke did not mention Simon any more, but the magician earned his negative place in history by giving his name, "simony," to the practice of religion for money, especially so-called religious magic.

On the way back to Jerusalem, Peter and his colleagues preached the gospel to many villages in Samaria and other places in Judea (v. 25). That in itself was significant progress. Peter went to Samaria simply to investigate. As he invited the Spirit to come to the Samaritans, he also allowed the same Spirit to work in his own heart. The investigator became the reporter; the spectator became the participant.

The Episode with the Eunuch (8:26-40)

Besides the fact that the conversion story of the Ethiopian eunuch is beautiful in and of itself, this episode is included in Acts because it marks another very important development in the history of the church. The eunuch is the first recorded Gentile convert. First orthodox Jews, then Hellenistic Jews, and now God-fearing Gentiles have come to faith in Christ. God was at work encouraging the spread of the church beyond geographical, religious, and racial perimeters. God did not direct Philip to the eunuch in order to have a Gentile convert; but in the process of receiving Christ, the eunuch did become the first Gentile convert. Luke recalled the episode to illustrate his point of the broadening ministry of the church.

The Spirit of God was helping Philip expand his gifts (v. 26). Already he had preached in Samaria, and now he was being led by an angel to another exciting spiritual rendezvous.

A God-fearing eunuch, high in the Ethiopian court, was returning to Ethiopia from a time of worship in Jerusalem (vv. 27-28). He served Candace, the queen, who, though the female consort, actually ruled the country. "God-fearing" is a rather technical term denoting a Gentile who believed in the God and ways of the Jews but who could not or would not fully convert to Judaism. This man would probably have been prevented from converting because he was a eunuch.

Philip boldly approached the official's regal chariot, heard the man reading aloud from the prophet Isaiah, and offered to help him understand what he was reading (vv. 29-35). Perceiving Philip to be a man of spiritual understanding and a Jew, the eunuch eagerly invited him to get up in the chariot and open the Scripture.

The Scripture was Isaiah 53:7 ff. "Who is the prophet talking about?" asked the sincere Ethiopian. Philip quickly identified the Suffering Servant of Isaiah with Jesus the Christ, the first time in New Testament theology such an identification was actually made. Everything Philip told the eunuch was good news. Whereas he had been excluded from the Temple because of his race and physical condition, in Christ the Ethiopian was cordially invited to come into the inner recesses of the presence of God. There were no barriers in this new faith; all shared equally in the grace of God and in the salvation offered by the Suffering Servant.

As they traveled, faith welled up in the eunuch (vv. 36-38). Coming upon a body of water, a wadi, he exclaimed. "Look, there is water. Since there are no barriers to faith, let us stop, and you can baptize me." By the side of the road, with dozens of soldiers, attendants, and probably some passersby looking on, this high official of government submitted himself to the rite of baptism as an expression of his newfound faith in Jesus Christ.

"When they came up out of the water" (v. 39) leaves no doubt concerning the mode of baptism: immersion. Only after some years had passed and the theology of the church was altered did the mode change from believer's baptism by immersion to sprinkling or pouring and then to infant baptism. While it is true that the attitude of the heart is more important than the mode of baptism, Baptists believe that immersion is the most accurate method of baptism to reflect the life, death, and resurrection of Jesus.

Since Philip's work was completed, the Spirit took him away as

quickly and as mysteriously as he had been sent. The next time
anyone saw Philip, he was in another city preaching the gospel
(v. 40).

Saul's Conversion (9:1-31)

We simply cannot make too much of the conversion of Saul of
Tarsus from the fiercest enemy of the church to its greatest spokesman
and theologian. All of world history has benefited from his Christian
witness, the exemplary and intense life he lived, and most of all his
legacy as a writing theologian.

With the exception of some information about Peter, the rest of
Acts revolves around the life and ministry of Saul, who came to be
called Paul. Even though the secular world often does not recognize
the significance of the conversion, it surely holds its place among
the greatest events in the history of civilization.

A Restless Spirit (9:1-2)

Not content to harass the Christians in Jerusalem, Saul received
permission from the high priest to go to Damascus to arrest and extra-
dite followers of the Way, both men and women, back to Jerusalem
for trial and judgment. Glad to have such a zealous advocate on their
side, the high priest and his cohorts gladly gave Saul the necessary
papers.

The picture is one of a terribly restless spirit knowing that something
was drastically wrong in his life, but unable or unwilling to admit
the reality or cause of the disorientation. To keep from exploding
from the inner pressure, Saul went madly charging around, grabbing
good and simple folk who had found peace with God through Jesus,
and clapping them in prison. There is no reason to believe that Saul
was a wicked man before his conversion, but he was painfully misdirected in his efforts.

The Visitation (9:3-9)

Frantically he pushed himself and his men toward Damascus, his
mind buzzing furiously with all the frightening thoughts that had

lodged there over these last months (v. 3). Jesus. Stephen. Signs and wonders. The innocent, gentle look in the eyes of most he had arrested. "Must hurry and get to Damascus lest word of my mission goes ahead of me and those I am seeking run and hide."

Suddenly, the light! Blindness. Confusion. His animal rearing and tossing him to the ground. His attendants and soldiers thrown into chaos. Then the voice—oh, that voice. He would never forget that voice till his dying day.

This was not the first time that voices from heaven had been heard. Jesus had heard those voices. Some Old Testament personalities had had vivid experiences with God. But this was surely the first time for Saul, and he was scared witless.

"Saul, Saul, why do you persecute me?" (v. 4). The voice was full of tenderness and gentleness, yet stern enough to convey unmistakable rebuke.

"Who are you, Lord?" (v. 5). "And what do you mean I am persecuting you? I am only trying to do my duty as a Jew."

Don't you imagine that Saul knew immediately who was talking to him? And he probably knew exactly what the Lord meant when he asked him about the persecutions.

After the light, the voice, and the blindness, the voice spoke again, telling him that his next step was simply to get on to Damascus and wait (v. 6). Meditation, contemplation, and reflection are part and parcel of any great adventure, especially a spiritual undertaking. Of course, Saul did not know he was about to embark on a lifelong missionary enterprise in the name of Christ; but God knew, and he designed those days in Damascus as preparation for the mission he had laid out for Saul.

The men who were with him were completely bewildered (v. 7). Apparently they did not experience the light; but they did hear a sound, even though it may not have been understood as a voice. As Saul began to get up from the ground, he discovered his blindness. The once proud Pharisee had to be led by the hand like a child (v. 8). For three long days and nights, with nothing to eat or drink (and probably no desire for either), Saul waited (v. 9). What emotions must have surged through that dynamic man during those days of blindness? Would he ever see again? Who was this Jesus he had been persecuting? What new and dramatic turn would his life now take? How quickly one's life can completely change directions!

A Reluctant Witness (9:10-17)

The gospel had evidently already come to Damascus. How ironic it would be if Ananias, the man commissioned to restore Saul's sight, had been a refugee from one of Saul's vendettas in Palestine or Galilee. In a vision the Lord told the good man of his responsibility to go to Saul, lay hands on him, and thereby restore sight to the former persecutor (vv. 10-12). Ananias would be expected because at that moment a parallel vision was being given to Saul.

Ananias had heard of Saul and the hard time he was giving the believers (vv. 13-14). "Lord, are you sure you want me to do this? That man has been your enemy."

"Ananias, trust me. Go do what I tell you to do" (paraphrase of vv. 15-16). And Ananias, a true saint of God, took a deep breath and set off for the street called Straight in Damascus, the oldest city in continuous existence in the world. It seems rather poetic that Saul's conversion and call to the brand-new should take place in and around the ancient of ancients. God maintains his own brand of continuity.

Healing came through the obedience of Ananias (v. 17). He was the immediate catalyst for unleashing the stupendous power of spirit and intellect locked up in Saul's twisted, angry, frightened soul. In his accomplishments Saul rapidly eclipsed Ananias, but where would the world be without men like this sensitive, obedient, courageous disciple? Every notable Christian leader I know anything about has had his share of Ananiases who have absolutely made the difference between darkness and light. Saul and his varying traveling companions/preachers turned the world upside down for Christ. Ananias may never again have left Damascus, but he played his strategic part in the extraordinary revolution wrought through Saul.

Moving in a Different Direction (9:18-25)

With the touch of the faithful disciple's hands, sight was restored to the blinded Saul (vv. 18-19). With sight came strength and determination. Baptism at the hands of Ananias must have followed immediately; then food was next.

To get his bearings and begin the process of sorting through the bits and pieces of the new life so dramatically begun, Saul remained in Damascus a few days, praying and talking with the disciples (vv. 20-25). There may well have been some painful moments for the former enemy of the church as he came face to face with men and women whom he had hounded out of their homes in Jerusalem or who had fled rather than face his uncontrollable wrath. I believe there was forgiveness from those fire-tested followers of Jesus. They may have had to think a moment before they spoke to Saul. But after one look at his face, freed and given peace by the risen Lord, their animosity simply had to melt away. Their cause was too important, Saul's obvious special place in the kingdom too paramount to waste much time and energy nursing grudges.

Although Saul's mind was calmed, his energy and zeal remained unabated. His direction was simply and powerfully turned around. Luke said that he immediately started preaching in the synagogues of Damascus, emphatically declaring, "[Jesus] is the Son of God" (v. 20). What a testimony to the changing power of an encounter with Christ!

And the change was not lost on the Jews of Damascus to whom he preached. As he preached with fire and compelling intellect, the men stroked their beards and puzzled, "Is this not the man who came here to stamp out the very religion he now proclaims?" Along the way those with a bit more brass doubtlessly chided Saul with that question. But he would not be deterred. Daily he was strengthened, sharpened in his preaching. He confounded the Jews, using the Scripture and the testimony of his own life to demonstrate that Jesus was the Christ.

So intent was Saul, so convinced, so brilliant, that leaders among the Damascus Jews quickly grew weary of him. They became so angry at him that assassination plots were secretly hatched to rid themselves of this troublesome fanatic. Saul's Christian friends got wind of the plots and hastily made plans to transport him out of the city by lowering him in a basket over the city wall. In all his finery, with soldiers and attendants, Saul set out from Jerusalem. He would have been wined and dined by the city officials in Damascus while he did his dirty work of rounding up followers of the Way. When his work was done Saul would have left as he came, with ceremony and the best wishes of Jew and Gentile alike. But Christ came into his picture, changing everything. He stumbled into town blinded by a light, had his sight restored by a simple Jewish follower of Jesus, preached not to praise but to mounting suspicion, and finally had to escape for his life under cover of darkness.

Blessed by Barnabas (9:26-27)

No wonder he was not welcomed by the young church in Jerusalem, this Saul, who but a few short weeks ago was their archenemy (v. 26). How did they know that he was not feigning discipleship in order to spring a massive trap on the followers of Jesus?

Barnabas, who had sold his property and cast his lot completely with the church, took the time to look deeply into Saul's eyes, talk with him, and get to know him. In the process he became convinced that the Christ of Calvary had touched this man and had indeed taken over his gifted life (v. 27). "I will vouch for him," Barnabas may have told the apostles and others. "Jesus, who saved you and me, who called us to our work, has also saved this man Saul and has commissioned him to be a missionary *extraordinaire* to the Gentiles." The Jerusalem believers took him in, but down the line we will see that some of them never overcame their suspicions of Saul. When he began to propose heretical changes in their patterns of thought, their worst fears were borne out.

Parenthetically, there is some debate about the exact sequence of events. Some scholars believe that Saul retreated to the desert for three years between his conversion in Damascus and this visit to Jerusalem, while others disagree. We will follow the sequence that Luke offered us.

Service Brings Steady Danger (9:28-30)

With his usual vitality, exhibiting little apparent concern for his life or for the shock to the total Jewish body politic his about-face must have triggered, Saul set about to preach all over Jerusalem (vv. 28-29). Naturally he ruffled some feathers, this time among the Hellenistic Jews—Jews who had lived in other parts of the empire but who, for various reasons, had come to Jerusalem to live. Their years among other nations and races gave them a different perspective, so they easily banded together in Jerusalem to form their own synagogues. We have noted that Hellenism had been a broadening experience for such disciples as Stephen and Philip. But evidently Saul got mixed up in groups of reactionary Hellenists who, at considerable sacrifice, had practiced their faith in alien lands and who, since moving back home, were not going to tolerate any diluting forces. Saul had not been preaching too long before these Jews were plotting to kill him.

For his own safety, members of the Jerusalem church arranged for Saul to flee to Caesarea and then take a ship for his home territory of Tarsus (v. 30). (Later on we will find Saul once again being spirited to Caesarea to save his life.)

Since we will travel in and out of Caesarea for the rest of our study, let's pause a moment and talk about this seaport town. Herod the Great reclaimed this ancient seacoast town, with careful engineering created a harbor, and generally built the town into a gleaming Hellenistic city. In honor of Caesar Augustus he changed the name from Straton to Caesarea. Beginning with the reign of Herod the Great, the city was the seat of Roman government in Judea.

So (Meanwhile) the Church . . . (9:31)

From time to time tiny words of overriding importance are inserted in the text. *So* or *meanwhile,* as *The New English Bible* translates the word, has an abundance of meaning. While persecutions were taking place, while theological debates were shaping up, while Roman armies marched, and while bearded judges in the Sanhedrin fulminated about gnats' hairs, the church was steadily gaining strength. Saul could have his conversation, Stephen even could die, the apostles could receive their beatings; but in it all, through it all, and in spite of it all, the church, momentarily catching its breath in the eye of the storm, was steadily built up—both from within, spiritually, and from without, numerically.

Even while some doctrinaire Jews and Christians debated the advisability and feasibility of taking their religion across racial and ethnic lines, common folk, the kind of folk who have always been the mainstream bearers of the gospel, quietly crossed those disputed lines. They told the good news that God had come in Christ. People in Judea, Galilee, Samaria, and beyond found new hope for everyday living and assurance of eternity with God. Walking in awe of the mighty acts of God and in the quiet assurance of the Holy Spirit, thousands surrendered their lives to the Son of God and began to experience the kingdom of God right where they lived and worked every day.

Meanwhile the church . . . through all the changes that two thousand years have brought . . . meanwhile the church. War, pestilence, theological wrangling, ecclesiastical schism, suspicion, prejudice . . . meanwhile the church. From stone wheels to steel-belted radials, from slave power to horsepower to atomic power . . . meanwhile the church. Emperors have come and gone, popes have reigned and died, denominations have flourished and then wilted . . . meanwhile the church.

And the gates of hell shall not prevail against the church. Hallelujah for the church. Hallelujah for the Christ of the church. Hosanna to God our Father, who in the Spirit continues to breathe life into and through the church.

Peter's Great Surprise: Gentiles Believe
9:32 to 12:25

The church was gradually spreading out, not only geographically but also racially. Philip had cracked the wall of partition that separated Jew and Gentile when he led the Ethiopian eunuch to faith and baptism. Peter had seen the half-breed Samaritans believe in Jesus and manifest the Holy Spirit. Peter's encounter with Cornelius and then his defense of his actions to the brethren in Jerusalem are key events in Acts.

Peter on the Coast (9:32-43)

Aeneas Healed (9:32-35)

During this lull, while Saul was catching all the heat, Peter toured some of the cities on or near the Judean coast (v. 32). Apparently communities of faith had sprung up in some of those towns, and Peter wanted to pay them a visit.

In the town of Lydda, located about halfway between Jerusalem and Joppa, Peter met Aeneas, probably a believer, who had been bedfast for eight years (v. 33). In the name of Jesus Christ, Peter instructed the invalid to rise and "make your bed." That phrase could also be translated "arrange your couch"—for example, "set your table for eating." At any rate, the man was healed and got up from his bed. Many in that area turned to the Lord because of the healing Peter had brought about.

Resurrection of Tabitha (9:36-43)

In the seacoast town of Joppa, Tabitha (Dorcas), a gracious, charitable believer in Jesus, fell sick and died (vv. 36-37). According to correct Jewish care for the dead, she was ceremoniously bathed and laid out in an upstairs room. There preparations would not take long because burial was usually done on the day of death.

News of Peter's healing of Aeneas had sped to Joppa. Peter was

sent for and came with the delegation from Joppa without any delay
(vv. 38-43). Heartbroken friends, especially widows who had been
recipients of Tabitha's generosity, stood around the bed weeping.
After dismissing the mourners, Peter knelt by her bed, fully aware
that healing would not come from him, but only through him in the
power of Christ. After praying, he ordered her to open her eyes.
She did so and immediately got up from her bier. There was much
rejoicing and no little fear and awe when the crowd saw Tabitha
walk out with Peter. More people believed in Jesus and attached
themselves to local communities of faith because of this mighty act
of God.

Peter stayed for many days with Simon, a tanner. Some aspects
of tanning would be unpleasant and unorthodox to a regular Jew,
but Peter stayed with the man nonetheless. Perhaps as Peter worked
through his uneasiness with the tanner, the Lord was preparing him
for the pivotal relationship with Cornelius and his soldiers.

Cornelius and a Major Breakthrough (10:1 to 11:18)

Biographical Sketch (10:1-2)

Centurions were the backbones of the Roman army. Nominally
in charge of one hundred men, their rank would equal that of a captain
in today's army structure. Secular history depicts them as stalwart,
sturdy, cool military leaders. The New Testament always speaks kindly
of centurions, perhaps because they dealt generously with the Jews.
The first recorded encounter between Jesus and a Gentile was his
meeting with a centurion (Matt. 8:5-10; Luke 7:2).

No one knows how Cornelius came to faith in God, but all indications
are that he was a God-fearing Gentile like the Ethiopian eunuch.
He believed deeply in the Jewish God and gave his money and support
to the Jewish causes, but chose not to formally convert to Judaism.
It is a sad but interesting note that while such a man would be deeply
devoted to God, the Jews would not in turn recognize him as a man
of faith. If orthodox Jews maintained a wall between themselves and
a bona fide proselyte, they would surely keep their distance from a
Gentile who chose not to become fully converted.

In spite of the condescension with which most orthodox Jews regarded him, Cornelius was faithful to God and to needy people. He had grown weary of the empty paganism of Rome. Perhaps in searching for a center around which to build his life, he had some sort of burning bush experience with Yahweh, God of the Hebrews. Yahweh's ethical monotheism, love, wrath, holiness, and righteousness spoke to the soul of Cornelius; and he became a believer.

Cornelius' Vision (10:3-8)

Perhaps while praying late one afternoon, Cornelius had a vision in which an angel from God appeared to him. His initial terror was eased when the angel called him by name and when he assured Cornelius that he had found favor with God because of his prayers and generosity to others.

The angel instructed Cornelius to send a message to Joppa, to the home of Simon, a tanner, requesting Simon Peter to come to Caesarea (vv. 5-6).

If we could ever doubt God's intentions to make salvation available to all people in every nation in every era, this one event should cancel the validity of such an idea. Already there had been encounters with Gentiles; but God wanted the head apostle, Peter himself, to see clearly the mandate to go into all the world.

Used to giving and obeying orders, the centurion sent immediately for three of his men, told them of the vision, gave them directions, and urged them to hasten (vv. 7-8). Excited beyond measure, he probably slept very little during the next hours, waiting for what God had in store for him through Peter's visit.

Peter's Vision (10:9-16)

At noon the next day, after a busy morning of preaching, healing, and debating with hardheaded Jews, Peter retreated to his host's house for prayer, rest, and food. On the roof of the house, while the meal was being prepared downstairs, Peter prayed and meditated. As he prayed, he fell into a trance (vv. 9-10). We are not sure of the nature of the trance—whether he dozed off, was "caught up" in the Spirit as others had been before him, or whether the revelation came to him with his eyes wide open. But the message was from God.

The heavens opened up, and something like a huge sheet was let down in which were placed all kinds of animals and birds, ritually clean and unclean (vv. 11-12). (Read Lev. 11 for a description of clean and unclean beasts. Clean creatures were suitable for human consumption, while unclean were banned.)

And then came an unnerving command from the Lord. "Peter, you are hungry. You have requested food. Kill and eat!" "No, Lord, you don't understand. I have never eaten anything unclean. Never in my whole life. I would rather die than take such food into my body" (author's paraphrase of vv. 13-14).

Why didn't Peter kill one of the clean animals? Because the clean animals had been defiled by coming into contact with unclean creatures. God was certainly building his case for the impending meeting with Cornelius. Then came the clincher from the Lord. "Peter, what I have said is clean is clean. Do not dispute my word!"

God was preparing Peter for what was about to happen to him. By this stage in his ministry, Peter's prejudices were likely wearing thin. Already he had had many startling encounters with Samaritans, Hellenistic Jews, and even some Gentiles. Those whom he had met, who had come to faith in Christ, gave undeniable evidence of a life-changing experience with Jesus—the same kind of experience that Peter was realizing. So Peter was making progress in working through his prejudices, but he was far from liberated. The fisherman would need all the spiritual help he could get as he dealt with Cornelius.

Using the animals as his illustration, God was declaring emphatically to Peter, "What I have said is clean is clean!" God created man and said "That's good. He's *clean*. Now, don't any man call another man unclean. Call him sinner. Call him wrong. Even call him evil. But do not call him unclean." Peter saw the vision three times (vv. 15-16).

The Men at the Gate (10:17-22)

Talk about timing! God's arrangements never go wrong. While Peter was struggling with the vision, trying to decide what it meant for him, knocking was heard at the gate downstairs. "Peter," the Spirit seemed to say, "you are puzzling over the vision. The answer is knocking at your door. Go, open the door, and receive your answer."

Two trusted servants and a devout soldier—Romans, Gentiles all, were standing at the gate of a Jewish home. Conflicting thoughts must have resoundingly clashed in Peter's mind—"Unclean!" "No, clean. Remember?"

If there was a moment of tension, an instant of indecision, Peter, the rugged fisherman, the growing, surrendering disciple of the Lord of the nations, dispelled the fleeting moment of awkwardness. "Come inside. Be my guests." He fed the soldiers and provided beds for them. For the first time Simon Peter, born a Jew, reared in Galilean synagogues, and taught that Gentiles were an abomination unto the Lord, ate a meal with Gentiles and slept under the same roof.

It must have been an awesome time for the fisherman. He was tested, but he passed with flying colors. Peter would have his relapses. Under pressure from colleagues in the Jewish church, Peter would back up a bit on this noble stand. But he never did go into full retreat.

Peter "Leaves Home" (10:23-33)

The day Peter left Joppa to go to Caesarea with the Gentiles, he left home. He left the home of Jewish prejudices to begin a lifelong journey into human relationships. From the text it would seem that Peter did not know why Cornelius had sent for him until he arrived at Caesarea. Perhaps for the first time he began to understand that this new faith he had been so boldly preaching to his fellow Jews might indeed be for all peoples.

When he got to Cornelius' house, a large crowd was waiting. To Peter's surprise and dismay, the centurion fell down and gave homage to the apostle. "No, no," Peter must have exclaimed. "Don't do this. I am a man *just like you.*" That in itself was quite an admission for the fisherman; but he meant exactly what he said.

After admitting the unorthodoxy and first-time experience of this meeting, Peter wanted to know what he could do for them. Cornelius related the vision he had concerning Peter. "Please, sir," requested the Roman after telling his story, "present to us all that God has commanded you."

Peter's Sermon (10:34-43)

Peter declared that "God is no respecter of persons" (v. 34, KJV) in that he offers himself to all men who will fear God and do what is right. He said that the Jews had no corner on God (v. 35).

Peter then related that God sent his word in Jesus Christ to Israel to preach good news and to heal. God gave Jesus a unique anointing as his word to the people (vv. 36-38).

In line with other examples of apostolic preaching, Peter told his Gentile congregation that even though Jesus did good and was well beloved, the Jews (meaning the leaders) slew him by hanging him on a tree. But he would not stay dead because God raised him from the dead. Peter declared his experiences with the risen Lord, relating Jesus' command to go and preach to all the nations; then he closed with his personal reaffirmation of Jesus as judge of the living and the dead and the one about whom all the prophets had been foretelling for centuries (vv. 39-43).

The Coming of the Spirit (10:44-48)

Peter's preaching, coupled with the willingness of the Gentiles, opened the way for the Spirit of God to come to Cornelius and his company.

The Jewish Christians who had come from Joppa to witness the encounter were utterly amazed to see the manifestations of the Spirit upon these Romans. "Why," they exclaimed, "the Spirit comes to them just as he did to us. Amazing."

When the Spirit came in such obvious power, Peter enthusiastically asked, "What is to prevent these people from being baptized?" Since no one even thought about objecting, they were baptized in the name of Jesus Christ and welcomed into the family of God as full brothers. The Romans asked Peter to stay with them and teach them more of Jesus and the new Way he was offering.

Peter's Report (11:1-18)

Reports of Peter's work with Cornelius reached the Jewish believers in Jerusalem. Rather than celebrating the marvelous ministry, many of them recoiled at Peter's contact with the Gentiles and attempted to call the apostle on the carpet for his actions (vv. 1-3).

Some of the believers in Jerusalem were beginning to see the universal implications of the gospel, but others were holding tightly to their old ways while attempting to embrace the new—placing new wine in old wineskins. The circumcision party was composed of those who held most tenaciously to their old ways. Peter was able to still the conservatives this time; Paul would debate with them later. But they never completely gave up and in their negativism may have contributed to the dramatic shift from Jewish Christianity to Gentile Christianity that later marked the internal life of the church.

This party's concerns were not just religious. Politics got into the picture. As long as the orthodox Jewish community regarded the believers as simply a branch of Judaism, albeit a renegade branch, persecution would not be too severe. But if word got out that the disciples were fraternizing with Gentiles, great fury would engulf the church.

The best defense was a full explanation. So Peter stood up and simply recounted all that had happened, starting with his own vision and ending with the coming of the Spirit to the Gentiles (vv. 4-18). When Peter explained that the Holy Spirit came to Cornelius just as he had come to them, all fell silent—some in agreement and affirmation, others in resignation and sullenness.

Barnabas and the Church at Antioch (11:19-30)

Preaching Fugitives (11:19-21)

None of those Jewish believers who had to flee their homes under the persecution of Saul were glad to have to run away and leave their possessions and maybe their families, but indications are that they did not waste much time lamenting their loss. They went to Phoenicia, Cyprus, and Antioch, preaching all the way to all the Jews they met (v. 19). Why just to Jews? They simply had not grown enough in Christ to preach to all they met.

Some hardy spirits among the fugitives, however, began preaching to Greeks also. These were Jewish believers who either were from Cyprus and Cyrene or who had come through these places on their way from Judea. Perhaps taking heart from Peter's work with Cornelius, they began to reach out to Gentiles in Antioch of Syria (v. 20).

Instant success! God had prepared many in Antioch for his message. By cooperating with the Lord, hundreds of people in Antioch came to faith in Jesus Christ and formed themselves into a strong church (v. 21). Indeed, this Antioch church quickly became a great missionary fountainhead. Further into the story we find Paul adopting the Antioch church as his spiritual home.

Barnabas to Antioch (11:22-24)

Reports of the overwhelming success of the gospel in Antioch came to the church at Jerusalem, which, in turn, sent Barnabas to investigate. Several times we will read of various leaders reporting to the church at Jerusalem. Although other congregations evidenced more service and vitality than the one in Jerusalem, it was the first church. It had emotional and historical clout beyond its numerical strength. James, the brother of Jesus, was the pastor of the church. In those early days the church in Jerusalem was regarded as the mother church. There is nothing to suggest that the church had actual authority over other congregations; rather, it served as a meeting place, a clearinghouse for doctrine and information.

Barnabas had been the special servant of that congregation, an emissary of sorts. No doubt he eagerly accepted the assignment to investigate the Antioch church, rejoicing when he saw God living in the believers in Antioch. It did not matter to him that the congregation was heavily Gentile. It did not matter that he had had nothing to do with their conversion or with the success of the church. Barnabas could be glad for the work of other people without jealousy. While he was in Antioch he exhorted the church members to be faithful. Because of his preaching, even more people came to faith.

Barnabas Enlists Saul (11:25-26)

Then a flash of inspiration or a brilliant illumination from the Holy Spirit reminded Barnabas of Saul over in Tarsus. Saul had escaped from Jerusalem, made his way to Caesarea, and then caught a ship home. We do not know how much time had elapsed or what Saul had been doing in the meantime; but when Barnabas showed up in Tarsus and invited Saul to come with him to strengthen the work in Antioch, the man from Tarsus packed his clothes, got a few books, and left posthaste. For a full year they labored together in Syria, preaching Christ, reveling in the response, and developing a glorious friendship.

An important footnote to the year in Antioch: It was in Antioch of Syria that the disciples were first called Christians. Since the Jews who came preaching and their Antiochene converts were always talking about *Christos*, the Greek form of the title *Messiah*, it was not long before outsiders were calling them Christ-people, Christians. The name fit; and from henceforth the followers of Christ would generally be called Christians.

Love One for the Other (11:27-30)

One of the gifts of the Spirit to the church was that of prophecy. Perhaps men who felt this gift banded together into a "school of prophets" reminiscient of such groups in the Old Testament. At any rate, a group of these men came to Antioch.

One of these, Agabus, predicted a famine which did occur. The church in Antioch, evidently spared the worst effects of the famine, collected funds which they sent to the mother church in Jerusalem for relief of suffering. Ironically, if some of the Jewish Christians in Jerusalem had had their way, there would have been no church in Antioch or anywhere else. Yet here is that very church sending money to those who had originally sought to limit the church to Jews only.

Wicked King Herod (12:1-23)

Biographical Sketch (12:1*a*)

The Herod of this episode is not to be confused with some of the other Herods who intermittently ruled in Palestine during the first Christian century. This Herod was the son of Aristobulus and Princess Mariamne (of a royal Jewish line) and the grandson of the infamous Herod the Great, who was on the throne when Jesus was born and who built the gorgeous Temple in which Jesus worshiped. When Herod the Great had his son Aristobulus murdered in 7 B.C., young Herod was whisked off to Rome both to get away from his grandfather and also to seek his fortunes in the imperial city. Through some twists of fate the young man, who happened to be in the right place at the right time, became a close friend of Gaius Caligula, who became emperor in A.D. 37. Since Herod had helped him to the throne and had remained a loyal courtier, the new emperor rewarded his Jewish colleague with the title "king" and over a period of a few years gave him large holdings in Palestine, including Galilee and Perea. When Caligula was assassinated and his uncle, Claudius, became emperor, the wily Jew was further rewarded by having Judea added to his holdings.

Even though the new king was a Herod, he still had Jewish blood in his veins from his mother's side of the house and was, therefore, more acceptable to the Jews over whom he was to reign. Smart enough to seize the advantage presented by the reasonably high regard in which he was held, Herod sought to further ingratiate himself by carefully keeping Jewish customs. The rites and rituals of the Jews may not have meant anything to the king; but, to keep up appearances, he went along with all their feasts and practices.

Murder for Fun (12:1*b*-3*a*)

Probably word got out that Peter, the leader of the apostles of Jesus, had eaten with Gentiles. This flagrant disregard of Jewish customs inflamed the Jews against the Christians and caused a stir in the land. Since the king was on a program of "getting along with the Jews," he took this occasion to further his cause with his subjects by persecuting members of the new sect.

In this wave of terror, James, the brother of John and the son of Zebedee, one of the "sons of thunder," was killed, apparently in a mob scene during the arrest. Time and again we painfully encounter the devaluation of human lives. For no reason other than to build up his own shaky throne, the king, with the encouragement of the so-called people of God, took human lives.

Jail Again for Peter (12:3*b*-19)

If James' death pleased the Jews, what would Peter's death do for the bloodthirsty crowd? The king ordered the arrest of the fisherman. Since Peter had the reputation of mysteriously getting out of jail, extra guards were assigned to watch the apostolic leader. The arrest came during Passover, so Peter languished in jail during the feast days, awaiting a mock trial and certain execution when the celebration was concluded (vv. 3*b*-4).

But the king did not reckon with the purposes of God or the power of prayer. The church in Jerusalem was in fervent prayer for Peter's safety and God heard those prayers (v. 5). It was part of his plan that Peter be released so that all of the king's security came to naught when pitted against the fervent petitions of God's people praying in the will and spirit of God.

In the middle of the night before Peter was to be publicly executed, another heavenly visitation came to Peter, loosed him from his chains, spirited him past sleeping guards, and led him safely to the street outside the prison. At first, the Scripture indicates, Peter thought he was having a dream from which he would awaken to find himself still in jail. But when the fresh air hit the apostle, whatever daze he was in quickly left him; and he rejoiced at his deliverance and marveled at the power of God (vv. 6-11).

It is interesting to note that the angel found Peter asleep. So strong was his faith in God, so confident was he in his relationship to Christ, that the night before his execution Peter could go to sleep on the floor of a nasty dungeon. The Scripture does not say so, but it is reasonable to believe that Peter's faith was fortifying him, whether for life or death. He wanted to live; but if the Lord wanted him to die as Stephen and James had done, the big fisherman was prepared.

Back to the upper-room house he sped. So much had happened in and around that house that it was only natural for Peter and other members of the church to gravitate to that place (vv. 12-17). Sure enough, the church was gathered there to pray for Peter's safety and for courage. Then an amusing thing happened. When Peter knocked on the door, Rhoda, a young Christian girl, went to see who was there. She got so excited when she saw Peter that she ran back into the house, failing to let him in, in her haste to tell the church that Peter was outside. The people did not believe her but accused her of being a bit daffy. When Peter continued to knock, he was finally admitted into the house amid the celebration of the praying church.

Peter quickly told his friends of his miraculous release, drew comfort from their presence and prayers, and left for another place, probably going into hiding for a while.

The church can be that kind of community to which we go first to share our joys and sorrows, victories, and defeats. As our churches become praying congregations, they can be havens of comfort and mutuality, where we can freely and securely share the good and the bad things that happen to us.

The guards could not have prevented the release of Peter if there had been ten thousand of them, but Herod in his madness had them executed when he was told of his prisoner's escape (vv. 18-19).

The Death of Herod (12:20-23)

Tyre and Sidon were ancient seacoast cities north of Palestine. Although they were wealthy trading centers, they were dependent on Palestine for many of their basic foodstuffs. Somehow the rulers of the cities had offended the vain and fractious Jewish king, and he summarily cut off their food supplies. Through Blastus, the king's adviser, they were able to bring about a truce (probably on the basis of a hefty bribe to the official), whereby food once again could be shipped to the troubled cities.

Perhaps in celebration of the restoration of relations between the twin cities and Palestine, a festival was declared; games were ordered; and all the people turned out to see the spectacle. In those days it took very little excuse to throw a day or a week of extravagant, bloody games where gladiators fought, wild beasts destroyed human beings, and public executions were cruelly conducted. Indications are that it was in such a glittering setting that King Herod, in all his finery, made a grandiloquent speech to the fickle crowd. Tradition says that the king was dressed in a resplendent robe made of genuine silver threads. The sun dancing off that gorgeous costume so dazzled the crowd that they declared, "He is no longer a man. He is a god!" Herod himself would not be above planting people in the crowd to scream such a declaration, which would quickly be taken up by the empty-headed crowd.

Immediately upon hearing the blasphemous cry go up from the mob, Herod fell forward and died, "being eaten up with worms" (author's paraphrase of v. 23). There has been medical speculation about the exact cause of Herod's death. Did he have a stroke? Did he have a devastating cancer that struck him a lethal blow that day? Was the blow a direct visitation from God? No one knows, but secular traditions agree with the Scripture that he either died that day or within a few days after having been stricken at the Caesarean games.

The ancients understood both natural and supernatural events like this to be signs and wonders from God. They would not have been troubled if a physician could have explained the exact cause of the death. What convinced them that it was the hand of God was not the cause but the timing. This view of the miraculous characterizes much of ancient Hebrew thought.

The Church Marches On (12:24-25)

Another of those little interludes that say volumes: The word of God met and moved beyond new frontiers constantly—frontiers of race, religion, geography, politics—every horizon known to man.

With Herod out of the way, persecution came to an abrupt halt, at least for the time being. Leaders of the church, such as Saul and Barnabas, gave a sigh of relief and thanks to God for ridding the world of one so thoroughly wicked, at the same time taking advantage of the restoration of peace to reorganize for further adventures.

All indications are that these two friends, along with young John Mark, a friend of Peter, left Jerusalem and returned to the church at Antioch of Syria. This brief respite gave them time to prepare for their greatest adventure yet—their first full-fledged missionary journey.

Paul's First Missionary Journey
Acts 13:1 to 15:35

Looking back on the story, we understand now that the church moved into a third phase of its life when Saul and Barnabas left Antioch for points west and north. If we had been living in those early days, we would likely have been totally unaware of any such things as "phases" in the life of the church; rather, we would have felt ourselves being moved along on the tide of events with a grand sense of immediate leadership of the Holy Spirit.

But phases were involved. The first phase was the work done in Jerusalem by the upper-room believers. The second phase unfolded when the seven Hellenistic Jews were elected to serve the church as deacons. The third phase, the one we will deal with for the rest of this book, came when Saul and Barnabas and their colleagues traveled to Asia Minor, supposedly to preach to Jews in those far-flung places. But when rejected by the Jews, they concentrated on the Gentile world. That shift pained Saul and his Christian colleagues, but it infuriated orthodox Jews who had despised the new Way when it was simply a part of Judaism and who now came to loathe the Way when it openly embraced Gentiles. These early Christian missionaries did indeed turn their world upside down for Christ. The last fifteen chapters of Acts deal with some of the details of the process of "upside downing" the Judeo/Graeco/Roman world.

This trip was another of those surprises. As we look at the text, we will discover a beautiful spontaneity, a freedom, a willingness to be led immediately by the Holy Spirit that we programmed Christians of the twentieth century long for but usually fail to grasp. The trip was born, not in a high-level strategy meeting in a denominational office but in the soil of the burgeoning Antioch church, with the Holy Spirit as the generative force, and the congregation as the midwife. Because those Christian pioneers had appropriated for themselves the luxury of no attachments and complete freedom of movement, when the revelation came to move out, they had but to pack a few necessary items for traveling, get together enough funds for the first leg of the trip, and sail away into the morning mists.

When we use the phrase "first missionary journey," we need to see clearly that this was simply Saul's first trip. Other unnamed witnesses may have gone traveling for the Lord. Nearly everywhere Saul went he found some Christians who had already been led to some knowledge of the Lord Jesus. True, in many cases their understanding was painfully partial; but at least they had begun their journey of faith and served as a nucleus for new work in those cities of Asia Minor.

The Antioch Church (13:1)

The Power of the Antioch Church (13:1a)

Through the rest of Acts the Jerusalem church holds the place of respect and prominence in the Christian movement, but the real power lay in the church in Antioch of Syria. This transfer of vitality is instructive. The Jerusalem church was fighting tenaciously to hold onto its traditions, to walk the tightrope between old Judaism and the new faith, to keep the high priest and his associates placated as much as possible. In the process of all this retention and compromise, the Jerusalem church gradually forfeited its right to leadership. On the other hand, the church at Antioch achieved the right by giving it away, thrived by risking, and gained influence by embracing a diverse membership in the city from all over the empire. Modern churches could learn a valuable lesson from that ancient story.

Antioch of Syria, north of Palestine, became one of the important commercial centers of the Roman Empire. Located on the Orontes River several miles inland from the Mediterranean Sea, the city drew to itself a substantial military outpost, a seat of Roman justice as well as a host of commercial enterprises. Such an international city automatically attracted people from all over the world. As some of these became followers of Jesus, they enriched the Antioch fellowship with their diverse cultural, geographic, and intellectual backgrounds. The nucleus of believers in Antioch welcomed these newcomers and capitalized on their varied experience.

Strong Leaders (13:1*b*)

In the church there were prophets and teachers. This division does not suggest offices nearly so much as functions. Prophets were those who preached on the basis of what they understood to be direct revelations from God through the Holy Spirit. Their messages would have been very direct, emphatic, and judgmental in the Old Testament tradition. On the other hand, teachers would have been people gifted in instruction both in the way to salvation and in the finer points of the developing Christian theology. They paid careful attention to Old Testament teachings that predicted and described the Messiah.

Among those people in the Antioch church were men like Barnabas, Symeon who was also called Niger, Lucius of Cyrene, and Manaen. We have already met the able and steady Barnabas. Some persons think that Symeon may be the same Simon of Cyrene, a black man, who carried the cross for Jesus. Some have tried to make this Lucius of Cyrene Luke the Gospel writer, but there is little evidence to support such a claim. Manaen, or Menahem, a foster brother of Herod Agrippa, was reared in the royal court of the tetrarch of Galilee and Peraea. It is ironic indeed when we reflect on the fact that these two men—reared together, exposed to the same teaching, given the same opportunities—chose such antithetical life-styles. Manaen became a noted Christian leader, giving his life in the service of the Lord. Herod Antipas shamefully sacrificed John the Baptist at the whim of his wicked wife and later refused to give justice to Jesus when the Galilean was dragged before him.

It is no wonder that such power and effectiveness flowed out of the Antioch congregation when we realize that strong men and women came to faith in and went out from this church.

The Call (13:2)

The missionary call came to Saul and Barnabas while they worshiped with the church. God has always worked through his church, regardless of the individual form a given body of believers may take. The faith passed on through the Lord's church is the undergirder of all our calls. The church is central to the entire flow of the Christian movement. Saul's call came in terms of, was conditioned by, and was interpreted through the church.

Fasting was a regular part of worship both in Judaism and in the Christian faith that grew from the shoot of Jesse. Jesus was quick to urge his fasting followers to do so privately, for their personal and spiritual growth, and not to make a show or splash.

The revelation that came was interpreted as being directly from the Holy Spirit. The revelation likely came through the total life of the Antioch church as it struggled to understand the dimension of ministry. Christian history is full of stories of such calls. The call of God to men by the Holy Spirit through the church—what a marvelous, divine plan for getting the Lord's work done.

The Commissioning (13:3)

When Saul and Barnabas heard their call, they were at church; and the congregation became a part of the total experience. To show their approval as well as to give their blessing, the congregation laid hands on the disciples and prayerfully, joyfully sent them out to their mission.

The Journey (13:4 to 14:28)

Cyprus (13:4-12)

Seleucia, the port city nearest to Antioch, lay some miles west of the city of Antioch on the mouth of the Orontes River. It was from this port city that Saul and Barnabas sailed for Cyprus (v. 4). Located as it is in the eastern portion of the Mediterranean Sea, this large island has always been of great military and commercial importance. Rome took over the island in 57 B.C. In 22 B.C. Augustus gave the island to the Roman senate as a gift. In the name of the senate, a proconsul administered the affairs of the island state. When the missionaries arrived on the island, Sergius Paulus was the senatorially appointed governor of the island.

Salamis, a Greek city on the eastern coast of the island, was a flourishing commercial center with a Jewish community large enough to require more than one synagogue. It was only natural for the Jewish missionaries first to approach their Jewish brothers and sisters in the various synagogues. Saul felt led (Rom. 1:16) to preach to the Jews first and then to go to the Gentiles. As his ministry unfolded, he became increasingly impatient with the Jews and steadily drawn to the Gentiles, though he never completely abandoned his commitment to the "Jews first" principle.

John Mark, Peter's protégé, accompanied Saul and Barnabas on the trip (v. 5). Some scholars believe that the missionaries, who were not eyewitnesses of the life and ministry of Jesus, relied on Mark as a resource person because he had personally witnessed significant episodes in the life of Jesus, especially his passion.

The eloquent preaching coupled with the healings that paralleled apostolic ministry attracted widespread attention (vv. 6-12). In due time Sergius Paulus, the governor of the province, summoned the missionaries to the palace for an interview. Saul and Barnabas were probably quite excited with this opportunity to preach to a Roman governor! But no sooner had Saul begun preaching than Bar-Jesus, or Elymas, as he was also known, began to interfere and heckle. Luke called the sorcerer a false prophet, not because he made statements that were false but because his whole approach to prophecy and ministry was fraudulent. Whatever revelation he may have claimed came not from God but from the devil. To add insult to injury, the man was a renegade Jew who had sold out his heritage for profit in the service of first one wealthy Roman "sucker" and then another.

Saul, never noted for his ability to bear fools gracefully, did not tolerate the venality of the magician very long. In white-hot anger the missionary turned on the heckler and in the name of Jesus inflicted blindness on him. Immediately his eyes clouded, and the wicked and now humiliated sorcerer had to be led from the chamber.

When Sergius Paulus saw this manifestation of God's power, he believed. What was the quality of that belief? Did the superstitious governor simply shift the focus of his fears from Bar-Jesus to Saul? Or did genuine Christian conversion come to the governor? We do not know. There are no more evidences of Christian activity on the part of the official, but extrabiblical tradition claims that the family of Sergius Paulus in later years became involved in the Christian movement in Rome.

Parenthetically, we can note that during the sojourn in Cyprus,

Saul apparently Latinized his name to Paul, by which name he is
called throughout the rest of his life.

Antioch of Pisidia (13:13-52)

The missionary entourage left Cyprus and sailed for the mainland
of Asia Minor, making port near the city of Perga (v. 13). It was here
that John Mark left the company and returned home. Why did he
leave? Was he afraid? Was he not comfortable with the ministry to
the Gentiles? Were there personality clashes between him and the
strong, even overbearing Paul? No one knows, but it is clear that
Paul regarded Mark's departure as a desertion. It is good that a rap-
prochement took place between Paul and Mark in later years, a testimony to the power of the reconciling gospel.

Antioch of Pisidia, one of several Antiochs in the Empire, was the
first major stop on this leg of the journey (vv. 14-15). This city near
the border of Pisidia was a Roman colony. Paul always attached much
importance to preaching in such centers since they were cultural
hubs of still larger areas. Obviously his strategy was to spend time
in these population centers, hoping that news of the gospel would
spread up and down the highways of commerce and trade.

In such a city as Antioch, naturally there would be a Jewish community. On the sabbath, Paul and his colleagues went to worship. After
certain prayers had been recited and the Scripture lessons read, Paul,
as a notable Jew in the congregation, was invited to bring the message.

Though Paul had been preaching constantly, verses 16-41 contain
his first recorded sermon. Paul addressed the men of Israel and the
God-fearers. (Remember that God-fearers were Gentile believers in
God, practicers of Judaism, but not full-fledged converts.) Paul emphasized that the Jews were chosen people, not because of their merit
but because of God's grace. He "bore with them" through all their
sins. In God's own good time he brought King David on the scene
to give glory to the nation, to honor God, and to be the ancestor
through whom the Messiah would come. Paul then emphatically declared that Jesus is David's heir and God's anointed Messiah.

In classical apostolic preaching style, Paul restated the major events
in the life of Jesus, giving emphasis to the rulers' refusal to recognize
Jesus as the Christ, scolding those officials for condemning the Lord
to die. Jesus' death, however, far from being a terrible accident, was
part of God's plan from the beginning, for by raising the slain Jesus

from the dead, God would incontrovertibly demonstrate the messiah-ship of Jesus of Nazareth.

Using commonly accepted messianic Old Testament Scriptures, Paul shored up his insistence that Jesus is God's anointed one. And then, joyfully, the preacher said, "We are glad to bring you this very good news: God has saved us and called us, and we are on his mission to you and to all peoples."

In the final verses of the sermon (38-41) Paul presented his grand theological principle that all men and women are justified by faith in Jesus Christ and given freedom "from which they were not freed by Moses."

He closed the sermon with an urgent warning to all present to believe and not reject this good news.

Many believed the message (vv. 42-43). Jews and God-fearers alike flocked to Paul and Barnabas to hear more of this incredible news. By the same token, many refused to believe. Luke says that jealousy was a factor in the official rejection of the message. Rulers of the synagogue could not stand to see so many of their people being drawn to the gospel. These leaders, like thousands more of their brothers and sisters, failed to see that Christianity was designed to be the con-summation of, and not the competition of, Judaism. Insecurity and unwillingness to be open to the new prevented Judaism from imbibing of the universal spirit of the way of Christ.

No doubt it came as quite a shock to Paul and Barnabas to feel the deep animosity and rejection from many of their Jewish kindred (vv. 46-49). If one had asked the missionaries ahead of time, they probably would have admitted anticipating some Jewish antagonism; but the vehemence of the rejection was so intense that they were pained and surprised.

Down but not out. "We turn to the Gentiles!" Tuck tail and run back home to Antioch of Syria because of opposition? Such a strategy never entered the missionaries' minds. Return to Jerusalem for consul-tation and fresh orders? Not on your life. "We will go to those who will hear." And they did. There was sadness and disappointment, but God's plan was larger than the Jews. To be sure, his plan included the Jews; but it was not limited to them.

If we remember that Antioch of Pisidia was the scene of the first recorded Pauline sermon, we can also remember this as the place where Paul and Barnabas were run out of town for the first time

(vv. 50-52). It would not be the last. In fact, they were run out of town just about as often as they left town on their own initiative. Symbolically shaking the dust off their feet against the Jews in Antioch, they scurried on to Iconium. But all was not lost back in Antioch. If the majority of the Jews hardened their hearts to the message, a host of Gentiles had eagerly and deeply embraced the new faith.

Iconium (14:1-7)

Iconium lay east of Antioch, part of the province of Galatia. Apparently Paul's anger at the Jews subsided on the walk from Antioch to Iconium, for the first place he preached when he got to town was the synagogue. Their preaching and teaching apparently met with instant and considerable success; many Jews and Greeks believed the message.

The missionaries had not been at work too long, however, before the familiar pattern began to emerge again (vv. 1-4). Unbelieving Jews grew uneasy with Paul's success and set about to undermine the work. Through lies, innuendos, and probably superstitions, these ruthless "sons of Israel" stirred up Gentiles and Jews alike against Paul and Barnabas. Apparently because Paul and Barnabas were so effective and so genuine, and because so many believed, it took some time for the opposition to fully gather itself against the missionaries. The tragic picture is one that shows the enemies of Christ working as hard against him as the friends of Christ were working for him.

In verse 3 there is a helpful insight into the nature of Paul's work. As Paul spoke boldly for the Lord, God authenticated the word of grace through signs and wonders. The inspiration to service is here. As we speak boldly for our Lord, he will honor and bless our efforts by allowing us to see fruit in the lives of people.

Finally, the uneasy truce erupted. The city became hopelessly divided, with some people supporting the work of the gospel and others ferociously opposing it.

The situation deteriorated so badly that plots were hatched to abuse and even stone the missionaries (vv. 5-7). Paul and Barnabas had broken no laws, but public sentiment was so violently stirred against them that mob mentality took over, endangering their lives and future ministry. Perhaps under cover of darkness, the two Christian disciples fled to another city—not surprised too much this time, however. Had not Jesus warned that he would come with a sword, dividing families, cities, nations? Paul and Barnabas went off to Lystra and Derbe, where new adventure and danger awaited.

Lystra (14:8-20)

Lystra, eighteen miles from Pisidian Antioch, was another Roman colony created by Augustus in A.D. 6. We do not know how long Paul was in town preaching before he met up with the crippled man, but as soon as Paul saw the man a bond was created between them (vv. 8-10). Such healings are beyond scientific or even theological understanding. Luke said simply that Paul looked deeply into the man's eyes and saw there the faith to be healed. Not every person with a handicap can or will be healed. Such healings always take place in the will of God. But in this case, restoration was in the purpose of God; and the man's faith was sufficient to complete the circuit of divine-human electricity. "Get up on your feet, man." And the man eagerly sprang to his feet, walking, jumping, even bouncing around. When had he last walked? Since the accident or the onset of disease? Maybe never? Jubilation!

So empty-headed were the people of Lystra that they hastily jumped to the conclusion that Zeus and Hermes had come to earth. Before Paul and Barnabas realized what was happening, a full-scale celebration was under way. The priest of Zeus seized on the uproar to get himself in the limelight. It is hardly believable that this man put any stock in the god he tended, but why should he miss such a ready-made opportunity to get some free publicity? In a matter of moments, it seemed, he was at the city gates with sacrificial oxen all bedecked in garlands, his holy knife poised for the plunge into the fat throats of the blank-faced animals.

"Wait," Paul and Barnabas screamed. "You are making a terrible mistake! We are men just like you." And with that Paul began to preach a frantic, impromptu sermon to the Lystrans, attempting to persuade them that it was God who had healed the cripple; that Jesus was God's anointed in whom they could find fullness and wholeness of life (vv. 14-18). Finally Paul at least stopped the sacrificing, even if he did not persuade many to faith in Jesus that day.

If the people could not have a party, they would have a stoning. Apparently Jews from Antioch and Iconium had come to town and were just waiting for an explosive situation like this to do Paul some harm. By turning the crowd's jubilation into embarrassed anger, the enemies of Paul fanned the worshipers into a lynch mob. Within a few seconds the apostle was left for dead under a pile of jagged stones. "There, that's the end of that!" the dissident Jews smirked. But it wasn't.

Backtrack (14:21-26)

His anxious friends gathered around the still form to mourn the apostle, only to discover that he was alive. Apparently, after a few minutes to let his head clear, Paul was up on his feet and going again. The next day, complete with cuts and bruises, the indefatigable preacher marched off to the city of Derbe with his friend Barnabas. After a successful stay in Derbe, the small entourage began to backtrack, strengthening the new churches as they went.

In a few short words Luke gave a grand pattern for Christian disciplining. The missionaries (1) strengthened the souls of the new disciples, (2) urged them to continue in the faith, and (3) forewarned them that their chosen pathway as followers of Jesus would be full of danger. No doubt, Paul's bruises were eloquent testimonies to all that he was saying, and served both to hearten and warn these Christians, living, as they were, in hostile territory.

Elders or pastors were appointed to lead the congregations. Though the Scripture does not say so explicitly, indications are that the congregations and the missionaries agreed together on who were to be their leaders. Perhaps the churches nominated and the missionaries ratified the men who were called out to give special leadership to these brandnew churches.

Report Time (14:27-28)

What excitement and anticipation must have been expressed by Paul and Barnabas as they approached Seleucia, the port city for Antioch of Syria. Never in their fondest dreams could they have hoped for the measure of success they realized on their first bona fide missionary journey. Nearly everywhere they made a stop, churches were planted, flourished, and bore much fruit. They had known the disappointment of rejection by their own kindred; there were bruises that still smarted to the touch; but the pluses so far outbalanced the minuses that the overwhelming emotion was one of celebration and gratitude.

Like wildfire, word traveled from Seleucia to Antioch that Paul and Barnabas had come home. No doubt dozens of their Christian friends streamed to the seashore to welcome the heroes home. In the midst of much embracing and backslapping and not a few tears of joy, the glad reunion of supporters and missionaries took place.

The Antioch church immediately gathered to hear the full report of all that God had done in and through Paul and Barnabas. It did not matter that the missionaries had been run out of town, verbally and physically abused, and even left for dead; God had been at work. Disciples and Antiochenes rejoiced and marveled that God would entrust his work into their hands.

Most newsworthy of all was the declaration that God had indeed opened the door of faith to the Gentiles. Even though many of the Antioch Christians were Jewish Christians, they could see that the new way must push beyond the bounds of a narrow Judaism to embrace all people everywhere. Though saddened by the rejection of the Jews, these Antioch believers were men and women of God's new order and jubilantly celebrated these important breakthroughs.

The Journey Precipitates a Jerusalem Council (15:1-35)

Wet Blankets (15:1-5)

It hardly seems fair to have such a triumphant adventure blunted by a theological fracas, but that was what happened (v. 1). Many Jewish Christians simply could not understand that the new way transcended Jewish ritual. To Gentiles, exulting in their new-found faith, these Judaizers, as they came to be called, preached a doctrine of grace plus works and faith plus circumcision. Not only was such a requirement unnecessary to the Greek Christians; the very idea of submitting to the rite was repugnant. Along with the decision to preach to Gentiles, this was the most critical issue the church would face during its adolescent days in the first century. Persecution from without they could endure with victory, but insidious undermining from within could easily and quickly wreck the new movement.

When these Judaizers hit Antioch, they immediately became embroiled in heated debate with Paul, Barnabas, and others who had worked with the Gentiles (vv. 2-3). After hours of argument, the decision was made to go to Jerusalem and convene the leaders of the church for a council. This issue had to be decided quickly. On their way to Jerusalem Paul and Barnabas passed through Phoenicia and Samaria, preaching as they went.

The Jerusalem church's welcome to Paul and Barnabas was correct but somewhat distant (vv. 4-5). In other places the disciples were joyfully embraced; here they were simply welcomed. The good, able, but provincial Jerusalemites still were not sure about Paul. Barnabas was not as formidable, but even he was largely an unknown quantity.

In spite of all that had happened through Philip, Peter, Paul, and Barnabas, plus hundreds of other unnamed disciples who had worked with Gentiles, the archconservatives among the Jerusalem Christians were not moved.

Debate (15:6-12)

After much debate, Peter rose to speak. Why had he not spoken earlier? Why had he let the arguing and debating run on so long without making his own position known? Even though Peter had preached to the Gentile Cornelius and had seen the centurion come to faith, there was still doubt in his mind. He recalled the mind-bending encounter with the Roman soldier. Finally he pleaded, "Do not put a yoke around the neck of our Gentile brothers." Then with sardonic humor, the big fisherman reminds his fellow Jewish Christians: "The very law you seek to impose on the Gentiles has actually been impossible for us Jews all these centuries. We have tried to keep every jot and tittle, but most of us know we have failed. Why shift our problem to the Gentiles?"

Then Peter gave one of those eternal gems of truth that men and nations can cling to for all time: "We believe that we shall be saved through the grace of the Lord Jesus, just as they will" (v. 11). We need look no further for the way of salvation. We can spend the rest of our lives plumbing the depths of the words uttered by Peter, but we can devise no other program for salvation. Nor need we try.

Peter sat down, signaling that it was time for Barnabas and Paul to speak. The two missionaries recounted all they had seen, heard, and personally experienced during their memorable journey: lives changed, cripples healed, a Roman governor converted, rejection by the Jews, the Lystran episode, but, all in all, general acceptance of Jesus as Christ. There was no doubt at all where they stood—freedom in Christ!

By Common Consent, a Decision (15:13-35)

James, the brother of Jesus, had come to be recognized as the leader of the church in Jerusalem. Jesus had not designated him leader, and he in no wise took Peter's place as spokesman for the twelve; but his relationship with Jesus, coupled with his obvious ability and sincerity, earned him the place of leadership in that local church.

After the debate and the testimonies, James gave his decision, which was subsequently ratified by the assembly (vv. 13-21). We look in vain in the New Testament for monarchial church government. There were some strong leaders such as James, Peter, Barnabas, and Paul, who did not hesitate to make their feelings and desires known; but they did not act by decree. There is the consistent picture of shared church government with leaders making important decisions in cooperation and consultation with the congregations.

Pastor James, speaking courageously and against the prevailing spirit of the Jerusalem church, suggested that Gentile Christians should not be weighed down with Jewish customs; but for their own souls' good health, they should abstain from consorting with idols, avoid all sexual unchastity, and eat nothing strangled. The admonition for sexual purity is an incontrovertible plea for living on a higher plane. The dietary regulations are attempts at compromise. It is as if James said, "We have freed you from circumcision. Help us save face a bit by observing these basic, painless food restrictions."

The decision pleased them all, and by common consent the council and Jerusalem congregation selected emissaries who would travel to the Gentile churches to give the word of liberation (vv. 22-29). Silas and Barsabbas, leading men from the Jerusalem church, were selected to carry the conciliar letter and to fully explain the council's decisions to the non-Jewish Christian congregations.

Antioch was the first recorded stop on this good news tour. After the congregation was gathered, Silas and Barsabbas read the letter, gave the details of the decision, and generally exhorted the people. Amid much rejoicing the Antioch group received the good news, breathed a deep sigh of relief, then went on about their business of leading their town to belief in Jesus (vv. 30-35).

Paul's Second Grand Adventure
15:36 to 20:6

The Jerusalem council marks the culmination of the first missionary journey and serves as the catalyst for the second grand Pauline adventure. The impetus for the second journey was the reading of the apostolic letter prepared by the Jerusalem council to the churches in Asia Minor. If Paul needed a reason to strike out again, the urgency to deliver the letter and interpret its intentions was all that was necessary.

Paul and Barnabas Separate (15:36-41)

Paul Proposes Another Trip (15:36)

After a period of rest and recuperation in Antioch, Paul was ready to go again. By nature not a person to sit still very long at a time, he probably quickly caught up on his sleep, felt strength returning to his weary limbs, and grew daily more anxious for the welfare of the churches he and Barnabas had started. When finally his energies could be contained in Antioch no longer, he burst upon Barnabas, saying, "Let's go see about our friends and their churches."

Disagreement over Mark (15:37-38)

Barnabas needed no persuasion. Though of a quieter disposition than Paul, Barnabas loved the work of the Lord every bit as much and was equally as anxious to see how the new churches were coping with their worlds. "Fine," Barnabas would have said, "let's go immediately. But I would like to take Mark with us. He and I have been talking a great deal, and he feels that this time he is fully prepared to go the distance with us."

But for some reason or combination of reasons, Paul did not want

Mark to go with them. His judgment about the young man's capacity
to make a meaningful contribution to their ministry may have been
in honest variance with that of Barnabas. Perhaps there was a personality clash between Paul and Mark. But whatever the reason, Paul and
Barnabas were in sharp disagreement. Failing to resolve both the
issue and the feelings, their only course of action was to separate.

The separation, though not caused by God, was certainly used by
God—whereas before there had been one team, now there were two
teams. It grieves us to imagine the pain that the two comrades experienced, but from all indication the gospel message was furthered in
spite of the disagreement.

Paul and Silas (15:39-41)

As Barnabas and Mark sailed into the sunset headed for Cyprus,
the curtain of Acts drops on them (v. 39). Some scholars believe that
in addition to the Mark problem, the contention between the two
men was Paul's intense concentration on the Gentiles, while Barnabas
could not completely leave his Jewish roots. If that is the case, we
can better understand how Luke, the Gentile, could so easily shift
his attention away from the Barnabas/Mark team to focus on Paul.

Not wasting any time, Paul sent down to Jerusalem for Silas, who
had proved himself an admirable and capable disciple on his mission
as courier for the Jerusalem council. Apparently Silas eagerly accepted
Paul's call to travel, and the two left immediately for Asia Minor
(vv. 40-41). Indications are that Silas was a Roman citizen, which gave
him extra protection under the law and would make traveling with
the trouble-prone Paul less complicated. Then, too, he was a bona
fide member of the Jerusalem council and could be of great help to
Paul in the battle with the Judaizers.

Selection of Timothy (16:1-5)

Timothy's Family (16:1-2)

At Lystra, where Paul had been stoned, he met up with Timothy,
a young Christian, son of a Jewish Christian mother and a Greek
father. Perhaps on the prior mission to Lystra, Timothy, his mother,
and his grandmother had come to faith in Jesus. During the interven-

ing time the young man had developed into a strong, dedicated, bright young Christian disciple. Luke says Timothy was well spoken of by people in the entire countryside, meaning that he had effectively exerted his influence in and beyond his hometown of Lystra.

Timothy's Accommodation for the Gospel (16:3)

Of mixed parentage and living out in the empire away from the strict codes of Jerusalem, Timothy had not been circumcised on the eighth day of his life as prescribed by Jewish law. The Greeks regarded the surgery as mutilation, a crime against the body; and the boy's Greek father may well have objected to a rite he found profoundly distasteful and unnecessary.

Paul knew the lack of circumcision could be a problem as they worked with Jews; so before Timothy joined Paul and Silas on their travels, Paul insisted on, and the young man consented to, the rite. Some could regard Timothy's accommodation as a considerable price to pay, but it was probably nothing more than an aggravation to the young man. He was ready to go with Paul, anxious to be of service; and a few days of physical discomfort would be a small price tag on such a large opportunity.

A Strong Partnership (16:4-5)

A friendship flowered between Paul and Timothy that lasted for the rest of Paul's life. Timothy was that devoted helper with the strength to stand tall on his own. On many occasions Paul sent his friend Timothy on crucial missions to deliver important letters, to soothe troubled waters, and to shore up shaky churches.

The Macedonian Call (16:6-10)

The episode of the Macedonian call is remarkable and noteworthy, not so much because of the geography involved but as a testimony to the leadership of and Paul's receptivity to the Holy Spirit. The gospel had already been preached in Europe before Paul and his friends crossed the Aegean Sea, but their energetic service in Macedonian cities gave great impetus to the westward spread of the Christian faith.

Prevented by the Spirit (16:6-7)

We are not sure of the exact location or sequence mentioned in verse 6. Scholars are agreed that the Asia that is mentioned is not the huge continental mass we know today as Asia. Rather, it was the limited Roman imperial province called Asia. The picture is that Paul wanted to go into that province and preach but was prevented by the Spirit. How did the revelation come? Some say it could have come from the mouth of a prophet, who plainly told Paul not to go in that direction. Perhaps it was a combination of political factors in that region. Or, most likely, Paul simply had one of those holy hunches by which the Spirit of God sometimes directs us.

Unable to preach in Asia, the small company prepared to go into Bithynia, but once again were prevented by the Spirit (v. 7). By now frustration and confusion boiled and bubbled in Paul and his colleagues, but new directions were coming. They would simply have to be patient and wait on the Lord. The Spirit had never misdirected Paul before, and he surely would not start now. Maybe one or all of the band needed a time to settle some issues. Success had showered on them. Some time of reassessment, a moment to understand that they were in the Lord's army, on the King's business, may have been just what was needed for the moment.

The Vision (16:8-10)

Deflected by the Spirit from going into Asia and Bithynia, the men went to the city of Troas (vv. 8-9). Some days after arriving in that town, Paul had a vision in which he experienced a Macedonian pleading for him to come over and help him. Macedonia, though technically comprising only the northern reaches of the Aegean Peninsula, in Paul's day was practically synonymous for all of Greece. Dating all the way back to the eighth and seventh centuries B.C., the region had been important in Greek history. It remained for Philip II and his son Alexander III (the Great) to lead their kingdom to dominate all of the Greeks. From Macedonia, Alexander moved out to conquer much of the world and to establish Greek culture as the prevailing sociopolitical force for at least three hundred years.

The rapid-fire language in verse 10 leads us to believe that Paul woke up from his dream, roused his friends, and immediately set about to make plans to go to Macedonia. It was a crucial development because at this point we have the first of the "we" narratives (16:10-17). Here and in other passages (20:5 to 21:18; 27:1 to 28:16) Luke used "we" to include himself in the story of Paul.

Luke was no idle, speculative bystander, loitering around on the fringes of the crowd, stroking his beard. No indeed. Along with Paul, he received the call from God to preach to the people in Macedonia. He stood ready with bandages and ointment to patch up broken heads and arms, but his primary function was to preach and teach the gospel. He did not simply stand behind Paul and Silas and Timothy; he stood with them, holding his own as a minister as well as a physician.

Philippi (16:11-40)

Lydia (16:11-15)

If not the next day, then as soon as possible, Paul and his company took a ship from Troas, across the northern neck of the Aegean Sea, to Samothrace, in those days a voyage of about two days. From the port of Samothrace they caught another ship that took them down the Macedonian coast to Neapolis, the port city for Philippi, which lay about ten miles inland (vv. 11-12). In keeping with his missionary strategy to focus on population centers, Paul headed for the city of Philippi, since it was the military, economic, and political center for that area. Philip II of Macedon had taken the village of Krenides, fortified it, and renamed it for himself.

Evidently there was no synagogue in Philippi. Paul, wanting to worship on the sabbath, located a small prayer group on the edge of town and joined with them (vv. 13-15). The group, made up mostly of God-fearing women, welcomed the missionaries, listened to their message, and eagerly embraced the faith. The leader of that prayer group was Lydia, the seller of purple cloth and dye who had come from the area of Thyatira to set up her business in Philippi.

As soon as she and her friends were baptized, she invited the missionaries to make her house their headquarters while they were in the Philippian area.

These people have the distinction of being Paul's first European converts, though by no means were they the first Europeans to become Christians. The eagerness with which they believed Paul's gospel and the decisiveness with which they entered fully into the Christian movement must have been of great encouragement to Paul and the others, who probably were still a bit uncertain as to why they were in this new part of the world.

Challenging Demons—Personal and Financial (16:16-24)

The unmitigated joy they felt from the meeting with Lydia was soon diminished by a slave girl who tagged along behind the missionaries, sarcastically taunting the men. She said, "These men [say they] are servants of the Most High God, who proclaim to you the way of salvation." This heckling went on for several days, and the girl's twisted mental condition manifested itself in utterances that made people believe she was telling their fortunes (vv. 16-17). Finally Paul could bear it no more and demanded that the tormenting demons in the young lady's mind come out. That very hour the girl was freed from her devils. But her masters, who greedily exploited her condition, lost their source of income and became furious at Paul. It made no difference to her owners that the girl was in deep misery, that she lived in the pits of hell and despair.

Seeing their young fortune-teller well and whole, and consequently worthless as a soothsayer, the owners set up a hue and cry that quickly resulted in Paul and Silas being brought before the two magistrates who judged the city in the name of the Roman emperor (vv. 18-24). Apparently with little or no judicial hearing, the two missionaries were stripped and beaten with rods. (*Rods* refers to a bundle of rods called fasces, bound together by cords and often having a battle axe inserted into the bundle, carried by "lictors," who were bailiffs and chastisers for the judges.) As soon as the two magistrates had passed judgment on the missionaries, the lictors tied their hands and beat them the prescribed number of times across their backs, then remanded them to a jailer who clapped them in stocks and locked them away in a cell in the town dungeon.

Songs at Midnight (16:25-28)

In spite of their aching backs and unmercifully cramped positions, Paul and Silas mustered the spiritual and physical stamina to sing, probably some of the new hymns that anonymous Christian writers had composed, while the other prisoners listened.

Suddenly an earthquake shook the place, and their bonds were loosed. As soon as the tremor hit, the jailer was immediately awake, rushing to see which of his prisoners had escaped. Seeing the door open, he jerked his sword from its scabbard and would have taken his life in automatic retribution for escaped prisoners when Paul shouted out in the dark, "Don't take your life. We are all still here."

What Must I Do to Be Saved? (16:29-34)

No one can know exactly what the jailer meant when he asked his question. Surely he did not understand the full theological implications of his question, and there is nothing to suggest that he knew anything about Jesus. Most likely while hustling them into their cell, arranging their stocks, and rough-talking the missionaries, he perceived something quite different about these two men. While they surely did not welcome their beating and imprisonment, there was a calmness and a security about these two Jews that the jailer had not seen before. Then when Paul not only stayed in his cell but managed to keep the other prisoners in theirs after the earthquake, the jailer knew he needed whatever these two strange, quietly powerful men possessed. So, if he was not asking a heavy theological, eschatological question, he was surely asking an intensely personal human question: "What must I do to be saved . . . as you two men are saved?"

Paul's reply, to the point and timeless, simple yet profound, answered the man's question in that moment, yet gave him a vibrant idea out of which he would live for the rest of his life: "Believe in the Lord Jesus, and you will be saved, you and your household."

Paul explained to the jailer and the other prisoners within earshot the Way of Jesus. The good news that filled the jailer's ears met the deepest needs of his own soul. In total disregard for the possible repercussions from the court, the jailer took Paul and Silas, his prisoners, into his own house, bathed their wounds, and eased their discomfort. After some more explanations from Paul, the Philippian jailer and his entire household believed in Jesus and were baptized. Amid feasting and much rejoicing, the jailer and his family celebrated their new faith in God through Jesus Christ.

Public Exoneration (16:35-40)

The next day the magistrates decided that Paul and Silas had sufficiently paid for the crime of disturbing the peace. So, quite casually, they issued an order for the prisoners' release (vv. 35-36). After all, the missionaries had been beaten with rods and locked up in stocks in the dungeon overnight. No doubt these two officials styled themselves as "fair men," so they would let the fanatics go with a stern warning to clear out of town right away.

"Not so fast," Paul told his new friend, the jailer. In all the confusion the day before, the magistrates would not listen to the insistent cry of Paul and Silas: "We are Roman citizens." Now Paul would gain some measure of protection for other new converts in Philippi and receive public exoneration for himself and Silas at the expense of the judges. By law no Roman citizen could be subjected to unnecessarily cruel punishment, especially until his crime was proved. The judges had not investigated the strident charges of the slave masters and had summarily, offhandedly ordered chastisement for the Jewish troublemakers.

Not only would Paul and Silas not leave the jail; Paul told the jailer to inform the magistrates that they would have to personally come to the prison and escort the wronged citizens out of their captivity, or Paul would tell higher officials of the hasty judgment. There was nothing else to do but comply; so the seething, nervous judges entered the prison, personally escorted the prisoners out, and told them to get out of town.

Paul and Silas did leave, but only after they had spent some time with Lydia and other new converts in the city.

Part of the significance of the conversion of the Philippian jailer is that this is the first recorded episode when a person, with no prior exposure to Judaism, an out-and-out pagan, became a believer in Jesus Christ. Luke used this true story to further illustrate his point that Paul was indeed a missionary to the Gentiles and that Gentiles, with no Jewish predispositions at all, could and would become believers.

Thessalonica (17:1-9)

Amphipolis, Appolonia, and Thessalonica (17:1)

Traveling the main highway, Paul and his company left Philippi, headed toward Thessalonica, and made brief stops, probably only overnight, in two towns along the way. Though Luke did not say so, preaching likely took place in these smaller towns; but in keeping with his strategy, Paul headed for the larger population center, Thessalonica (the modern city of Salonika), then as now, the main city of Macedonia.

The city had been founded in 315 B.C. on the site of a much more ancient village.

In the Synagogue (17:2-4)

Even though he had a fairly clear picture of what would happen to him, Paul, following his custom, went to the synagogue first and began preaching. His approach here was to show the Jews that it was necessary for Christ to suffer and die. Since the Jews had longed for a king, with an army to restore Palestine to the Jews, it would take some high-powered convincing that Jesus, crucified by the Romans (over whom he should have ruled), was the Messiah. Making extensive use of the Old Testament, he reasoned and argued both the necessity of Jesus' death and the reality of his resurrection.

Typically, many believed the message, while many more refused to accept the gospel. Among the converts were Jews, God-fearers, Greeks, and "not a few of the leading women."

Trouble from Those Who Refuse to Believe (17:5-9)

The orthodox Jews in the synagogue were jealous of the response Paul received to the preaching of the gospel. These Jews, like their kindred all over the Roman world, could not understand that the Christian faith was meant to be a fulfillment, an extension to their ancient faith, and not a rival religion. However, as the Jews refused to believe and constantly stirred up trouble for the new congregation, polarization did occur and forced Christianity to become a religion on its own.

There is another sad dimension to this jealousy. The synagogue had become a closed society, keeping out the very nations to whom God had called the Jews to minister. These jealous Jews were saying in effect, "If we will not be successful, you Christians can't either." This kind of petty bickering among church groups did not die with the close of the first Christian century.

It seems that there was always a crowd ready to boil into a mob. These jealous Jews inflamed the passersby; and before anyone knew what was taking place, the mob descended on the home of Jason, where Paul and company were being lodged. When the crowd discovered that Paul was away, they manhandled Jason and others in his house, venting their anger on the innocent hosts of the missionaries.

"The troublemakers have come here," the ringleaders of the lynch mob cried out to the city officials. Then to further catch the judges' attention, the mob accused Paul and his friends of serving and advocating a God who claimed he would someday be king.

Though obviously disturbed, the authorities kept their heads and refused to mistreat Jason and the others, simply taking a bond from Jason to guarantee Paul's good behavior. Breathing a great sigh of relief, Jason and his family were released.

Beroea (17:10-13)

The Difference in Beroea (17:10-11)

Paul's friends in Thessalonica waited until dark and then spirited the missionary and his friends out of town. This undercover flight was an old story for Paul by now. He and his friends made their way to Beroea, a city somewhat off the main highway. We do not know why Paul went to that town, but his subsequent experience proved his choice a good one.

Luke described the Beroeans as "more noble than (the Jews) in Thessalonica." What made the difference? In the case of Beroea *vs.* Thessalonica we do not know; but most of us would readily admit there are differences in communities, just as there are in churches and families. Some groups are open, willing at least to examine new ideas and change, while others are closed before the new idea is even presented. Some churches are friendly and outgoing, while others are cold and reserved.

One ingredient of the Beroean corporate life that stands out is their willingness to examine Paul's preaching, not on the basis of mindless prejudice but on the sure ground of the Scripture. Anytime we let the Scripture be our guide, our foundation as well as our judge, we are on solid footing. We may not always like what we discover in the Scripture, and we do tend to resist the mandates of the word of God; but at least we nearly always know where we stand and what to do.

Outside Agitators (17:12-13)

Not content to hassle Paul in Thessalonica, when the Jews from that city heard of the success of the gospel in Beroea, they scurried after Paul to stir up trouble and thwart the work in Beroea. The

Thessalonian Jews found just such a street-corner rabble in Beroea and inflamed them into a noisy mob.

Athens (17:14-34)

Paul Is Escorted to Athens (17:14-15)

Attempting to throw pursuers off their track, Paul's Beroean friends feigned a flight to the sea, then abruptly turned south and hurried the apostle on to the city of Athens. After getting Paul settled in the ancient city and receiving his admonition for Timothy and Silas to come with all haste, the Beroeans left the missionary to his own devices and returned to their homes.

The City of Athens (17:16)

Athens was already many centuries old when Paul paid the city a visit. For over five hundred years Athens had reigned as the queen of cities, the brightest spot intellectually, culturally, and architecturally in the western world. Statues dating from the golden age of Pericles (fifth and fourth centuries B.C.) dotted the city. The Parthenon crowned the Acropolis. In the cool marble porticos (stoas) that adorned the city, all manner of philosophies were discussed all day long. Most notable among the philosophical schools were those of Zeno (Stoics—taken from the *stoa*, where they met for discussion) and Epicurus. The Stoics, with their rather stern view of life, and the Epicureans, with their more liberal and temporal perspective, provided the philosophical and theological poles between which the thinking people of Athens moved.

Athens was no longer a political power, but Rome had the good sense to appreciate the depth of learning centered in the city, perceived the fierce commitment to freedom that lay stoking beneath the facade of marble and easy living, and decided to leave the city alone to basically run its own affairs.

To the people of Paul's day, the statues and monuments represented and actually embodied pagan gods. Even though Paul was supposed to be resting in Athens, waiting for his friends to arrive, he walked through the city. When he saw all those idols, his Judeo-Christian blood began to boil, grieving and offending his sensitive spirit.

Paul Tackles the City (17:17-21)

Before he knew what he was doing, Paul was into arguments with Jews in the synagogue, with God-fearers, and with anyone else he could engage in conversation (v. 17).

It was inevitable (and maybe even part of Paul's plan) that the leading philosophers who frequented the marketplace would take notice of him. Whether one was Jewish or Greek, he did not talk with Paul very long before the man's overpowering personality, intellect, and learning became evident. The sophisticated scholars were confused about the apostle (which was nothing at all new), some calling him just a babbler, other regarding him as a preacher of foreign gods, and still others acknowledging his brilliance (v. 18).

Probably after only a very few days, Paul was invited by the intelligentsia to come to the esteemed Areopagus, a court of sorts, and present his case. This was a signal honor for Paul, since only the most learned lecturers and scholars were actually invited to address this court, whose main job it was to determine religion and philosophy (vv. 19-21).

When we read their invitation to Paul to come and present his case, it is difficult to believe that any of the philosophers had any notion of embracing the new religion. Luke rather sarcastically commented that all the Athenians wanted to do was sit around and debate the latest philosophical or theological fad.

Paul's Sermon (17:22-31)

Like few sermons ever preached, this Pauline statement has been examined and criticized. Some scholars have said Paul failed to reach the Athenians for the gospel because he tried to be too rational and philosophical. Others have criticized him for the absence of Old Testament Scripture in the body of the sermon. Still other New Testament experts sing the praises of this sermon as the first statement to an entirely pagan audience, insisting that it is a marvelous setting of the simple gospel message in language that modern, sophisticated men could comprehend.

Paul acknowledged that Athenians were very religious. Indeed, countless religions were represented among the Athenians—so much so that Athens and religion were synonymous terms in the minds of many people of that day. And just to cover themselves in case any god or religion had been left out, some sensitive Athenian soul had built an altar to the unknown god.

Paul set about to identify for them that unknown god as the one God, creator of the world and of heaven. Drawing from his treasure trove of Jewish thought, yet not mentioning Judaism, Paul insisted that this one God could not be contained in a building or in any man-made shrine. Because he is complete in himself, he does not need sacrifices and oblations. All men are equal in the eyes of this God who gives life, breath, and "everything" to everyone. Toying with the Athenian myth that they were unique, that their ancestors literally sprang from the earth around the city, Paul declared that this God whom he represented is the father of the human race and the controller of history and destiny, even going so far as to set the boundaries of human habitation in given periods of history.

Because much of their theology put the gods in faraway places such as the mythical Mount Olympus, Paul invited them to enter into a relationship with this God who was nigh unto them. "He is not far from each one of us" (v. 27).

Arguing from man back to God, Paul said that since man is not made of silver or gold, it is not reasonable to believe that the God who made us, whose offspring we are, is made of silver or gold or is a creature that can be fashioned with the hands of men.

As Paul brought his message to a close, he said in effect: "Now let's get serious about this. You people sit around and philosophize about one fad or another. God says it is now time to settle down, repent of your sins, and prepare for judgment that is coming in the person of the man (Jesus) whom God has appointed. Come live!"

Then came the clincher that brought Paul's discourse to an abrupt halt: the resurrection from the dead. The man whom God had appointed to be the judge of the earth and through whom hope would be infused into life had been killed, but God raised him from the dead. The party broke up on that statement.

The rationalism of the Stoics precluded any idea of resurrection. They had heard of the idea before; resurrection talk was not at all confined to the Christian faith. But such a phenomenon seemed too far out for the cold logic of the Stoics. And the Epicureans, with their emphasis on pleasure for pleasure's sake, who generally gave in to their whims, counted on death as the final arbiter, the final accountant. The Epicurean could have his good time because the grave was coming and would end all life. These Epicureans wanted no part of any talk of resurrection.

Paul's sincerity, his intelligence, and his command of the learning of his day might have been beginning to get to some of those philosophers in the Areopagus. If that were the case, these men would have welcomed the chance to cut off Paul's sermon.

The Typical Mixed Reaction (17:32-34)

Some of the Greeks scoffed, while others believed. One who did believe was a member of the inner circle of Areopagites, a man named Dionysius. We can hope that he used his influence and witness to spread the good news of Christ and his resurrection.

Corinth (18:1-17)

The City of Corinth (18:1)

Corinth holds the reputation of "bad child" among ancient cities. Always important as a naval and commercial center, the city was noted for its independence, its vigor, and its immorality. In 146 B.C. the Roman general Mummius, in a savage act of revenge on the city for an anti-Roman revolt, razed the city to the ground so completely that the site lay abandoned for one hundred years. In 46 B.C. Julius Caesar refounded the city in honor of himself. It did not take long for Corinth to completely restore itself to a place of prominence and power among Roman provincial cities, finally designated as the capital of the Roman province of Achaia (Greece) in 27 B.C. With its revival in economics the city also experienced a rebirth of its old licentious ways, thanks to the worship of Aphrodite and one thousand temple prostitutes.

Paul maintained a lover's quarrel with the church in Corinth. The Corinthian letters show his affection for the people and for the city itself, but no other church gave him as much trouble and grief as did the congregation at Corinth.

As Paul approached the old but new city, he would have been fully aware of her history, at least generally cognizant of the problems that awaited him there. But the city met his requirement of a key population center, and as such he would invade it with the gospel. Before he was done, Paul spent approximately eighteen months there, established a strong Christian community, and effectively honored the Lord with his witness.

Priscilla and Aquila (18:2-3)

God's gifts of friends—what a treasure. Sometime after arriving in Corinth, Paul had the good fortune and blessing of God to meet Aquila and Priscilla, tentmakers by trade from Pontus by way of Rome. By reading between the lines, we can conclude that Aquila and Priscilla were from families of means in the region of Pontus in Asia Minor. Speculation is that their trade, tentmaking or leatherworking, led them to Rome, perhaps to establish branches of the family business in the imperial city.

Secular historians, contemporaneous with New Testament times, back up and expand on Luke's statement that Claudius ordered the Jews to leave Rome, but add "because of disturbances instigated by Chrestus." Obviously Christ was not in Rome, so he could not have stirred up the trouble. Scholars believe that the Jews, in an uproar *with* Christians *over* Christ, triggered riots and provided the anti-Semitic emperor with sufficient reason to run many of them out of Rome.

Indications are that Aquila and Priscilla became Christians before they left Rome, since Luke did not mention any sort of conversion experience in their lives after they reached Corinth. Paul heard about them, sought them out, joined them in their work, and became their dear friend in the process. They were admirable people and scholars of the new faith.

A Vision of Assurance (18:4-11)

Paul worked at his trade during the week, talked with people who came and went in the shop, and discussed the faith with the people on the street as he walked about. Every sabbath in the synagogue he argued about and pleaded for the new way as revealed in Jesus Christ.

When Silas and Timothy arrived from Macedonia, they found Paul completely absorbed in preaching the gospel (vv. 5-6). Since the faithful followers in other places had gathered an offering for Paul (2 Cor.

11:8; Phil. 4:15), the apostle was able to quit his job as a tentmaker and devote full time to preaching and teaching.

The content of his message to the Corinthians was the basic story that Jesus is the Christ. From other sources, especially the later Corinthian letters, we are able to see that Paul purposed to lay aside all attempts at philosophical arguments and stick to the basics.

Paul was getting older and less patient with the Jews. When they not only refused to believe in what he was saying but began to revile him, he determined to tolerate them no longer. In anger he employed the ancient symbol of shaking out his garment against the unbelievers and informed them that no longer would he bear any responsibility for their souls' salvation (vv. 7-8). He had done his part by preaching to them, by arguing with them, and by doing his best to love them—all to no avail. He left the synagogue to find another place in which to preach and teach. He did not have to look long or walk far. The house next door to the synagogue was available; so, without missing a stroke, he simply took over the house of Titius Justus.

An even more stinging blow was in store for the Corinthian Jewish community. Not only did Paul move next door to them to do his preaching; but Crispus, who had been one of the elected leaders of the synagogue, found faith in Christ and joined Paul's church.

Just because Paul moved out and led one of the leading Jews to Christ did not mean that the Jews were giving up on their program of harassment. Indeed, indications are that the aggravations only increased (vv. 9-11). Life was difficult for Paul, even though his message was falling on eager and open ears. The Lord sent one of those visions that had marked rites of passage for the apostle in times gone by. Through the vision, God urged Paul to persist, not to fear, because no physical harm would come to him. In addition, Paul was assured that his labors would bear much fruit because many people in that city would turn in faith to Jesus Christ and become followers of the Way.

Paul gained new strength to keep up the battle. For eighteen more months he labored for the Lord in the wicked city of Corinth, seeing hundreds come to faith in Jesus as the Christ.

Vindication (18:12-17)

If Paul thought that life would be a rose garden after God's vision of assurance, he was wrong. Instead of easing up, the Jews seemed to intensify their attacks on the apostle and on his converts (v. 12). The Lord had not promised ease; he had only promised the freedom from physical attack.

Finally the Jewish leaders in Corinth were able to haul their dispute before Gallio, the proconsul of the province, who agreed to hear their dispute (vv. 13-16). The fact that the Jews were able to secure an audience with the governor suggests that the man, an esteemed Roman from the noble family of Seneca, was new on the job. Determined to rid themselves of their gadfly, these Jews probably hoped to persuade this new ruler to decide against Paul and his religion.

More was at stake than meets the eye. Christianity was regarded by Rome to be but an extension of Judaism and thereby a legal religion. If Gallio had agreed with the Jews that Paul was preaching a new religion, the faith would have been in serious trouble with the Roman authorities. Only as a part of Judaism was the faith exempt from emperor worship and other repugnant Roman demands and rituals. If the governor had pronounced Christianity illegal, fierce persecution would have been unleashed on the fledgling churches before they had gained sufficient strength to withstand the onslaughts.

A wise man, Gallio probably knew exactly what the Jews were attempting. The synagogue leaders made their hysterical, strident charges against Paul and the new religion, demanding his ouster from Corinth. But before Paul could open his mouth to say a word of defense, Gallio impatiently interrupted, "You men are just mouthing words. This is an internal matter. Go settle this yourselves. I will not waste my time on this any longer."

To add insult to injury, Sosthenes, successor to Crispus as ruler of the Corinthian synagogue, was beaten as he left the courtroom (v. 17). Did irate Jews tear into their leader, making him a scapegoat for their humiliation at the hands of the governor? Or did anti-Semitic Gentiles take out their prejudice on the hapless Jewish ruler? No one knows for sure.

When Paul wrote his first Corinthian letter, he talked about a man named Sosthenes who had become associated with him in the work of Christ in Corinth. Could it be that this was the same man? Indeed, tradition has it that Sosthenes, like his friend Crispus, left the closed synagogue for the open church.

A Time of Hopscotching (18:18-23)

Sailing for Syria (18:18-21)

Capitalizing on the affirmative action of Gallio, Paul remained in Corinth for several more months, working day and night for the cause of Christ. He met with acceptance and success on every hand while battling with the disgruntled Jews, who still smarted from the slap in the face given by the governor. Then, perhaps, all the strain, anxiety, and hostility came crashing in on the apostle.

Suddenly he was filled with a desperate longing to go to Jerusalem for worship, then go to Antioch to rest and generally regroup his mind and body. Priscilla and Aquila, always ready for a new adventure, readily agreed to accompany him at least as far as Ephesus. So, within a few days, the matter was settled. Amid tears and warm farewells, Paul and his company left the Corinthians with whom he had fought, whom he loved with all his life, and with whom he would keep a running lover's quarrel going for years to come.

At the seaport town of Cenchreae near Corinth, Paul cut his hair "because he had a vow" (v. 19). In ancient days a man could take a Nazarite vow on the basis of which he agreed never to cut his hair or to drink wine. Samson's parents agreed that the lad should be reared a Nazarite (see Judg. 13:2-7). In Paul's day the duration of the vow had been modified so that a man could take a Nazarite vow for a lesser period of time, but the period had to last at least thirty days. For some reason, before he left Corinth, Paul had taken such a vow. Now that he was sailing for Jerusalem and the appropriate time had elapsed, Paul cut his hair, saved the locks, and probably offered them on the altar at the Temple in Jerusalem.

At Ephesus Paul's friends Priscilla and Aquila unpacked and set up shop, either a branch of other shops in other cities or simply a relocation of their Corinthian business. Ephesus became home for some time for this remarkable mobile pair of missionaries. Paul made a brief visit to the synagogue in Ephesus but declined the offer to stay for an extended time, promising them he would return in God's good time (vv. 19-21).

On the Move Again (18:22-23)

From Ephesus Paul sailed to the Judean seaport of Caesarea. Although Luke did not say so, the implication is that Paul immediately made his way to Jerusalem. In all of this there is an incredible feeling of hurry and haste. Was Paul trying to attend a festival celebration in Jerusalem? Was there a crisis in Jerusalem or in Antioch that craved his attention? If he was on a vacation, it would not be "unPauline" for him to hurry through even his time of rest and recuperation.

His worship in Jerusalem completed, he sped on to Antioch of Syria. But in Antioch something happened to at least slow down the journey. Some writers believe that it was during this unexpected delay in Antioch that Paul wrote his Galatian letter. Likely a trusted friend such as Timothy had met Paul in Antioch with the disturbing news that Judaizers, those who insisted on making Jews out of Christians, were extremely active in the churches in Galatia. In frustration, anger, and hurt Paul may well have penned his urgent apostolic letter to the Galatian churches, upbraiding them for allowing themselves to be duped into diluting the pure gospel that he and other bona fide disciples delivered to them.

The letter completed, Paul set off by foot on a trek through cities and towns where he had previously worked, strengthening churches and disciples all along the way. Though the exact route he took is open for debate, there is little doubt that he walked that great distance, preaching and teaching along the way, always heading toward the great city of Ephesus, in which he was determined to establish a new beachhead for the gospel.

Apollos (18:24-28)

Apollos from Alexandria (18:24)

Alexandria, Egypt, was the home of a large colony of Jews, some of whom had lived there almost since its founding by Alexander the Great in 318 B.C. We have already noted the spread of the Christian faith in all directions after Pentecost. Egyptians were among those in Jerusalem when the Spirit came in such power on the day of Pentecost, so it is not difficult to imagine that Apollos was converted to Jesus under the teaching of some unnamed Jew who experienced the empowering of the church firsthand.

Living away from the Holy Land, filled with a longing to finally return to that sacred place under the leadership of God's Messiah,

Apollos would have been particularly well versed in Old Testament prophecies concerning the advent of the Anointed One. When friends and/or family members came rushing back from Pentecost in Jerusalem, eagerly chattering about the strange events they saw and felt, Apollos would probably have been but a boy. The white-hot words of his elders burned their way indelibly into the mind and spirit of this brilliant young Jewish boy, striking a chord that he did not forget. In time, under the leadership of men and women who had come to believe in Jesus as the Messiah, deep faith flowered in this young man. Before too long one can imagine that he was himself preaching in the name of Jesus in an ever-expanding ministry of evangelism.

Partial Understanding (18:25)

What he knew he knew very well. When he came to Ephesus to preach, he must have caused quite a stir because of his power and eloquence. But he preached from only partial understanding. Luke said he knew only the baptism of John

This gap in his theology confuses us. How could he know so much and yet know so little? We have to remember that communication in that day was slow and laborious. The Jews who came back to Alexandria from that Pentecost experience would have been told about John the Baptist simply because he was a hero to the Jewish people, murdered as he was by the wicked, godless Herod Antipas. His preaching, baptizing, and rebuke of the king had entered into popular folklore. Those same Jews who revered John could understand the Baptizer's role in pointing toward Jesus as the Messiah, himself a victim of the Jewish political establishment.

But whereas they knew a great deal about John through popular storytelling, they would not have known too much about the fine points of Jesus' ministry and theology, primarily because the Nazarene was less flamboyant and eye-catching than the Baptizer. Simply stated, Apollos could believe in Jesus as the Messiah without knowing much about his life and ministry. Hence, he knew about John's baptism of repentance, anticipation, and preparation; but he just had not been told of Jesus' baptism as a testimony of fulfillment and as a living symbol of the resurrection. The resurrection he knew about; the baptism representing the resurrection he did not know about.

Let us be deeply grateful for the two thousand years of church history and doctrine on which we build our lives and faith. Indeed, our responsibility is even greater than those first-century believers around whom so much of the new was exploding. It is a testimony to the grace of God that they knew so much about their new faith and Lord, as scattered and out of touch with each other as they were.

Taught by Priscilla and Aquila (18:26)

When Apollos began to preach and teach in the synagogues in Ephesus, naturally Priscilla and Aquila heard him. Immediately they recognized his considerable gifts and reveled in his eloquence, but winced at the gaps in his theology. Rather than stand up and publicly rebuke him for his ignorance, indications are that they took him under their wing, invited him to their house, and instructed him in the complete ways of the Lord—explaining to him, no doubt, the meaning of Jesus' baptism and the coming of the Holy Spirit.

Effective Ministry in Achaia (18:27-28)

After a stay of unknown duration in Ephesus, Apollos wanted to go over to the province of Achaia to preach. Achaia comprised most of southern Greece below the province of Macedonia. Priscilla and Aquila and others in the Christian community in Ephesus encouraged him to go, probably helped him with funds, and gave him letters of introduction to Christian groups already at work in Achaia. The brilliant young Alexandrian preacher was welcomed with open arms by the grace-filled believers in Achaia, and together they were able to do a marvelous work for the Lord.

Ephesus (19:1-41)

Paul Completes the Understanding of Some Ephesian Believers (19:1-7)

Whatever had detained Paul in Antioch of Syria was settled, or at least attended to, and the incredible missionary set off on foot for Ephesus, preaching and strengthening churches and disciples along the way (v. 1). Some months earlier when he had rushed through Ephesus, leaving Aquila and Priscilla there to begin their work and witness, Paul had promised the Ephesian church he would return if at all possible. Never one to go back on his word, unless prevented by the Holy Spirit, the apostle steadfastly set his face toward Ephesus. In due time he arrived in that queenly city, so important as a cultural, economic, and religious outpost in the Roman Empire. Rome had made Ephesus the provincial capital for that part of the world and had also allowed Ephesus to exist as a free city-state managing her own affairs as an independent entity.

Central in the city was the temple of Artemis, regarded by many as one of the wonders of the ancient world. Before Paul was done in Ephesus he and his friends would have a ferocious battle with silversmiths who made their fortunes selling statues and trinkets to devotees of the pagan goddess.

Powerful though it was, Paul was not at all intimidated by the city; rather, he was thoroughly challenged by the scope of the work that beckoned to him as he neared Ephesus. The best indications are that he spent two productive but painful years in that place, experiencing some notable achievements as well as some monumental hurts, disappointments, and narrow escapes.

For some reason, Luke did not give all the unpleasant details that accompanied the successes that marked Paul's ministry in Ephesus. Primarily from the Corinthian correspondence we learn of the sufferings experienced by Paul at Ephesus. In addition to the riot and fanatical Jews mentioned by Luke, Paul had some terrible depression and disappointments; he was imprisoned with Andronicus and Junias (Rom. 16:7); there is even the suggestion that he was thrown into a beast-filled arena but managed to escape unharmed (1 Cor. 15:32). Even though he labored long and hard in the city, evidently he did not have a great deal of confidence in the quality of the work because later he would warn the Ephesian Christian leaders that "fierce wolves" would come to scatter the church (Acts 20:29-30).

Soon after he arrived in the city he met some disciples. We know nothing of these believers except they did not have the whole story of Jesus, but Paul attempted to complete their understanding of the Savior.

Even though their understanding of the faith was less than complete, Paul accepted them as believers in the Lord (v. 2). They admitted a lack of knowledge of the Holy Spirit, but their lives gave abundant evidence of his activity in their lives. Paul's opportunity was to identify the incredible spiritual force who was rearranging their lives on a daily basis, who was giving them new vitality and ability to cope with their world, who was empowering them to live a victorious, witnessing life in a terribly difficult world.

Since they knew nothing of the Holy Spirit, Paul asked the new believers about their baptism (vv. 3-7). Sure enough, they had received baptism preached by the followers of John the Baptist, a baptism of repentance, but they did not know about Jesus' baptism of faith and fulfillment, a baptism depicting the hope of the resurrection. When Paul explained the fullness of Jesus' baptism they requested rebaptism, which Paul readily granted to them. Then after prayer and laying on of hands, the Holy Spirit came to them and those excited believers manifested the classical Pentecostal expressions of the Spirit: tongues and prophecy.

Paul's Ministry in Ephesus (19:8-20)

Some people never give up, and Paul was one of them. It made no difference that he had had trouble in nearly every synagogue in Asia Minor—indeed had been run out of most of them. He kept trying. He had a deep desire to see his fellow Jews come into their full heritage in Christ and, in spite of their persistent rejection, he went back and back and back (vv. 8-10). Ephesus would be no exception. For three months Paul pleaded and argued with the Ephesian Jews about the kingdom of God. This use of the phrase "kingdom of God" is rare in Acts. Paul was preaching a kingdom of God in which Jews and Gentiles had equal standing before God. Such a message was more than the Jews could take. They disbelieved Paul's message so intensely that they began to revile the apostle, to blaspheme the very Way of Christ. When Paul could take their insults no longer he moved out, just as he had done in Corinth, this time to a nearby lecture hall owned by a man named Tyrannus.

For two years he preached the gospel there and throughout the province so that "all the residents of Asia heard the word of the Lord " (v. 10).

This break with the synagogue in Ephesus marks a painful phase in the development of the church. For years Paul and others had tried to work within the synagogue, hoping against hope that the Jews would believe in Jesus as the Messiah and embrace their Gentile neighbors as fellow disciples. From this point on the rupture between Jews and Christians, between synagogue and church, rapidly widened, so that by the close of the first Christian century what could have been one grand, all-inclusive fellowship had forever separated into two frequently battling institutions.

While the Jews were refusing to believe the message, many Gentiles were not only coming to saving faith in Jesus Christ but were being helped and healed by Paul as God used him (vv. 11-12). The handkerchiefs and aprons mentioned by Luke in verse 12 probably refer to articles Paul had used as sweat rags and aprons while working at his trade as tentmaker. So powerful was the activity of God in Ephesus during those days that marvelous healings and exorcisms were effected by the application of these clothes on a troubled person.

For us moderns this can be a troubling passage. Most of us have seen on television or heard on radio the pitches by so-called healers who urge listeners to send in for a certain kind of prayer cloth or amulet which is guaranteed to relieve all manner of bodily and mental distresses. In nearly every case the troubled listener is urged to send money along with his request for the minister's prayer cloth. Nothing like that is suggested in this passage. We need to note that this apron and sweat-cloth therapy was the exception rather than the rule. There is one example of a woman touching the hem of Jesus' garment and receiving healing, but that is a one-time event in the Gospels. Healing, when it comes, is always the work of God, in keeping with his larger purposes for the kingdom of God and for the individual. Not everyone who prays for physical healing receives physical healing. The granting and withholding of such healing remains a mystery with God in heaven. We must not build our personal faith in the Lord Jesus on the basis of physical healing or the lack of it.

This account of the healing by cloths and the following episode with the wicked exorcists is set in this paragraph as a polemic against magic. Magic is an attempt by man, through ritual, incantation, and charms, to manipulate the forces of the universe, whether they be divine or natural. The Christian faith must never be identified with cheap magic. Some people unwittingly regard prayer, for instance, as a form of magic. But praying in faith means that we say *Yes* to God whether or not he grants us the exact thing we think we need.

Whatever healing and exorcism took place was done not in the name of Paul of Tarsus, but in the name of Jesus Christ, Son of God. Paul understood that as a fact and time and again conveyed his deep feelings to the people with whom he worked.

This next episode (vv. 13-17) is actually funny if we see what really happens. A group of fake Jewish exorcists who claimed to be sons of one Sceva, whom they declared to be a high priest (no such high priest ever existed, according to the best records) traveled around the empire, purportedly casting out demons. They watched Paul work and heard him cast out demons and do healing "in the name of Jesus." "If that name works for Paul why wouldn't it work for us?" they reasoned. The next time they confronted a man who seemed to be possessed by demons, they commanded the tormenting devils to come out "in the name of Jesus whom Paul preaches." "Jesus and Paul I know," the demon declared, "but who are you?" Suddenly the possessed man leaped upon the seven scoundrels, beat them with superhuman strength, tore their clothes from their bodies, and sent them reeling naked into the streets of Ephesus.

To further celebrate the victory of true religion over magic, Luke recorded the memorable scene when many citizens of Ephesus who had practiced magic and soothsaying burned their books and completely forsook their attempts at the magical arts (vv. 18-20). Books of any kind were expensive items in those days, but books of magic would have commanded a handsome price indeed. So complete was the repentance of those magicians that they burned up thousands of dollars' worth of magic books.

In every way, in spite of the painful break with the synagogue and the subsequent harassment by the Jews and other nonbelievers, Paul's work in Ephesus resulted in a mighty strengthening of the work and word of God.

Looking to Rome (19:21-22)

These two verses are probably editorial devices Luke used to summarize several major events about which we learn from other Pauline sources. For instance, the Corinthian church was giving Paul a hard time. Several scholars believe that not only did Paul send Timothy to Corinth to stabilize the church, but Paul himself made at least one quick journey to Corinth. As we have noted, during Paul's more than two years in Ephesus he wrote the Corinthian letters trying to get those troubled and troublesome Christians on the right track. Also during his stay in Ephesus, the Christians of the provinces gathered a considerable offering that Paul planned to deliver to distressed saints in Jerusalem, whose faith in Christ was bringing them under economic ban from the establishment. Not only would the offering help relieve suffering in Jerusalem; it could make for a better feeling between the Jewish and Gentile Christians.

Having spent several years in Asia Minor Paul began to look more and more westward. He wanted to go to Rome, not to establish work there, because the Christian movement already had a firm hold in the Imperial City. He just wanted to go to Rome to preach and see for himself what God was doing there. Indications are that his long-range goal was to pass through Rome and head for Spain, which beckoned as a new frontier.

Luke said that Paul made all these plans and dreamed all these dreams "in the Spirit" (v. 21). Here is a key insight into the man and the way he operated. He was not afraid to push his mind and energies through all sorts of barriers, but he was careful to make his moves in terms of the leadership of the Holy Spirit.

Of course, he must go first to Jerusalem to take the offering, but in the meantime he sent two helpers into Macedonia to strengthen the churches.

Episode with the Silversmiths (19:23-41)

As long as Christianity stayed over in its corner, the pagans in Ephesus did not get alarmed (vv. 23-27). After all, that era in history saw the proliferation of new religions, with some setting up headquarters in the key city of Ephesus. The rub came when the Way of Christ became so pervasive that sale of trinkets, amulets, miniature statues, and other objects of worship for the goddess Artemis was threatened. When religion attacks the pocketbook of any established power group, conflict is just around the corner.

Paul and his friends had been so effective in the campaign to win the Roman province of Asia for Christ that many people had become believers, forsaking Artemis and her craftsmen in the process. Demetrius, apparently a leader among the silversmiths, became so agitated over the financial threat that he inflamed others in the guild to a riotous protest against Paul and the other Christian leaders. No matter how pious Demetrius may have sounded, his primary concern was economics—he and his fellow silversmiths were losing money and it was time to do something drastic to correct the situation.

Artemis had been worshiped in that part of the world for centuries. Not exactly the same as the Roman goddess of beauty, Diana, she was regarded in popular mythology as the mother of men and gods. The gorgeous temple in Ephesus housed "the sacred stone that fell from the sky" (v. 35), which was most likely a meteor that had fallen from the sky in antiquity. Some say the stone resembled a female figure with many breasts. Others say the stone was the focus of worship, but that a statue representing the many-breasted goddess had been struck and that along with the stone it held a prominent place in the temple. With eunuch priests and numbers of prostitute-priestesses the worship centered around fertility rites with strong sexual overtones.

Demetrius and his money-hungry guildsmen whipped the idle people into a nasty mob, urging them toward the city amphitheater where they would stage a full-blown riot. Along the way they grabbed up two Macedonians, Gaius and Aristarchus, traveling companions of Paul's, and dragged these two innocent Christian leaders into the middle of that howling mob. Note that Luke said that many of the people running around and making noise did not know what the scene was all about.

Alexander, a leader of the Jewish community, was shoved to the rostrum with the urging from his own people to make a speech against Paul. But when the man began to speak and the crowd realized he was Jewish, they only shouted him down with cheers of "Great is Artemis of the Ephesians!"

Finally, the town clerk, the chief administrative official of the free city of Ephesus, was able to quieten the hysterical mob. He warned them they were about to get him and the entire population into big trouble with the Roman officials, who would not tolerate such a scene lest it boil up into open rebellion against Rome. Ephesus held its free-city status in the good graces of Rome; therefore, feelings against Paul or for Artemis must not be allowed to jeopardize their treasured self-government. The steady voice and wise counsel of this respected official calmed the people. He reminded them that there were legal ways to handle their legitimate grievances against Paul and the other Christians. Court was held on a regular basis and they had but to prefer formal charges to get a hearing on the matter at hand. The power of that one lone voice prevailed, the crowd slowly dispersed, and a terribly explosive situation was defused.

Never underestimate the power of one voice for good or evil. In the home, church, community, office, many people really want to hear a voice that will call them to the right, the good, the noble. Nearly every time someone speaks up, someone else will respond.

To Greece Again (20:1-6)

Productive Visit to Greece (20:1-3a)

When dust from the nearly disastrous riot by the silversmiths had settled, Paul called his disciples in Ephesus together to preach and to exhort them to faithfulness one more time before telling them good-bye. After traveling around in Greece (Achaia) for some months, he settled in Corinth for the winter months. Many scholars believe it was during these cold days of winter (A.D. 56-57) that Paul wrote his great Roman Epistle, preparing the way for what he hoped would be a pastoral visit to the Imperial City. While strengthening the church or churches in Corinth and doing his writing, Paul also coordinated the collection of the offering he wanted to take to Jerusalem to relieve the suffering of the mostly Jewish Christians there.

Eluding a Plot (20:3b-4)

Just as he was about to board what may have been a "pilgrim" ship full of Jews headed for worship in Jerusalem, Paul and his friends uncovered a plot on the apostle's life. Indications are that once at sea, Paul would have been murdered. Since plots were by now old hat, but never to be taken lightly, Paul simply changed his plans, journeyed by land to Macedonia, and sailed from there.

Paul was not traveling alone; indeed he seems to have gathered men from representative churches of Asia Minor to accompany him to Jerusalem, share in the presentation of the collected offering, and give the Jewish Christians in Jerusalem further exposure to their Gentile brothers in Christ. By the same token, the Gentiles would have a chance to meet Jewish Christians, experience them as they lived under fire, and worship in the proper sections of the gorgeous Herodian Temple, which reflected much of their spiritual heritage.

Rendezvous in Troas (20:5-6)

The traveling companions went on ahead of Paul to wait for him in Troas. Paul, who had evidently been joined by Luke, remained in Philippi until after the Passover before setting sail for the rendez-vous in Troas. Perhaps Luke had solicited relief funds from Philippi and its environs and would accompany Paul and the others on to Jerusalem as the Philippian representative as well as physician and friend to the apostle. Luke would not be far from Paul's side for the rest of that fateful journey to Jerusalem and would be a constant companion from Jerusalem to Caesarea and eventually to Rome. After the season of Passover, Paul and Luke sailed for Troas, where they stayed for seven days in final preparation for the trip to Jerusalem, which the resolute disciple felt compelled to make.

To Rome (with Interruptions)
20:7 to 28:31

If a journey of a thousand miles begins with the first step, Paul took his first steps toward Jerusalem (and Rome) and his ultimate sacrifice for Christ with that seven-day visit in Troas. The nearer he drew to Jerusalem the deeper he felt the drawing power of God toward that city and the more urgency he felt about his pilgrimage.

Hastening to Jerusalem (20:7 to 21:14)

Troas (20:7-12)

This mention of a gathering "on the first day of the week" (v. 7) is the first clear statement of Christian worship on the first day of the week. Sunday worship was not originally intended to supplant the Jewish sabbath. For the Jewish Christians the orthodox sabbath remained a sacred day and would be so for approximately one hundred years. For Gentile Christians, to whom the sabbath was just another day, it was only natural to remember the Lord on the day of his resurrection. The mention of breaking bread doubtless refers to the love feast, a fellowship meal, in which was incorporated the reenactment of the Last Supper.

Since he was leaving the next morning by ship, Paul spent all the time he could with the Christians in Troas, talking far into the night. With what pleading, eloquence, theological depth, and intensity he must have exhorted those faithful friends. He had led many of them to faith; they were names and faces to him; he loved them deeply and sensed he would not see them again this side of eternity. It is no wonder that he gave them all he could in those remaining hours.

Eutychus, a young believer, maybe even a slave, sat in the window of that upper chamber (vv. 8-12). The combination of the late hour, the long speech, the smoke from the torches or lamps, and the possibility that the young man had worked all day proved too much for Eutychus. He dozed off, lost his balance, and fell to the ground from the third-floor window. The entire congregation rushed outside, expecting to behold a broken and lifeless body. Sure enough, there he lay, apparently dead from the fall. But Paul examined him and said, "Do not despair. He is not dead. Life is still in him." And to their complete amazement the boy was still alive. As you would expect, there has been endless speculation. Was he actually dead? Did Paul bring him back to life? Or was the breath simply knocked out of him by the fall, so that when Paul moved him the breath came back to him? Who knows? The event did not unduly alarm the congregation. When life and/or breath came back into the boy, the people reassembled in the hall, broke bread together, and picked up where Paul had left off.

Because the ship was to sail at daybreak, Paul finally quit talking. But even then he let his friends go on ahead while he stayed for a bit more time with his friends in Troas.

Sailing (20:13-17)

The geography of that part of the world was such that Paul could walk just about as fast as the ship could sail from Troas to Assos. At Assos, Paul boarded the coastal ship that skirted the rugged shoreline, putting in at major towns and cities along the route—a sort of "commuter" boat. Since he was attempting to reach Jerusalem by Pentecost, he decided not to go all the way to Ephesus. Instead, when the boat made port at Miletus, about thirty miles from Ephesus, he sent word into the city asking the leaders of the Christian community to come to Miletus to see him, which they readily agreed to do.

Farewell Sermon to the Ephesians (20:18-35)

This is an unusual passage (vv. 18-21) in that it is the only recorded address that Paul made to Christians. His other sermons had been delivered either to Jews or to Gentiles, but Luke has included only this message from all that Paul delivered to believers. It contains both exhortation in the faith as well as defense (apology) of the faith. Some scholars say Luke simply gathered lines from other Pauline material to write the speech. It is true that it sounds very much like some of Paul's letters, but the best evidences are that Luke actually heard the sermon, was deeply impressed by it, and in later years reconstructed the speech when he compiled Acts.

The first verses are a reminder of Paul's conduct, style of ministry, and devotion while he was in Ephesus. He had nothing of which to be ashamed and had caused his friends no embarrassment because of his personal behavior during the two years he lived in their city.

His opening statement offers a model of ministry for all of us: (1) He served with humility, even tears, enduring trials; (2) he taught the whole truth not holding back the unpleasant and judgmental, as well as exhorting them in the delightful and affirming; (3) he taught in public as well as on a one-to-one basis; (4) all he met were urged to repent and turn in faith to the Lord Jesus—Jews and Gentiles alike.

He sailed to Jerusalem bound by the Spirit of God (vv. 22-23). As long as he was bound by his own drives, ambitions, fears, and prejudices he was restricted, even choked off, from the best of his gifts and abilities. In surrendering to the bondage of the Holy Spirit he was granted the incredible freedom to exercise the best of who he was as a human being and as a Christian disciple.

The Spirit was propelling him to Jerusalem even though he was warned in every city that imprisonment and even death awaited him there.

He could honestly say that he did not value his life above the calling God had given him (v. 24). What really mattered was to do the will of God, to answer his call to the fullest extent, to do what the heavenly Father had prepared for him to do. Surely he did not devalue his life or human life in general. Paul himself testified abundantly in other writings that the final word about human life was not death but life—that God in Christ was striving to bring us to fullness of being both in this life and in the life to come, but we must not cling to physical life when the call of God might lead us even into mortal danger.

To sum up his speech (vv. 25-31), the apostle said in effect, "I have done all that I could for you. Now it is up to you." With ineffable sadness yet with triumph he could say, "You will see my face no more (this side of heaven) but that's all right. You have strength and resources to make your own way. So do it." He warned the Ephesian leaders that "fierce wolves" (v. 29) would invade and harm the flock. False teachers would come along who would try to gather personal followings. They must be on the alert.

Tucked away in this passage is a challenging statement. Paul could honestly say, "I did not shrink from declaring to you the whole counsel of God" (v. 27). It is not difficult to say the encouraging, uplifting words that are found in abundance in the Scriptures. It is not as easy for most of us to remind friends, families, congregations, and most of all ourselves, of the stronger and weightier mandates from the Word of God. Christian teachers must deliver the whole word of God, the positive and the negative, the soothing and the corrective.

In verse 32 comes a beautiful benediction. Paul commended his Ephesian friends to God and to the word of his grace, which was able to build them up and to bestow their full inheritance as members of the Christian community. Then he reminded them (vv. 33-35) that everyone must earn his own way. Even when he could have received remuneration for his services, Paul chose to work at his trade of tent-making lest anyone accuse him of trying to extort money from the Ephesians among whom he worked. Note that Paul did not say a minister should not be paid a salary for a full-time ministry. In other places he did accept love offerings from the churches to enable him to devote full time to his work.

On this subject Paul quoted the Lord: "It is more blessed to give than to receive." We serve the Lord not for personal reward but to know the joy of giving away our lives and money. Paul knew the truth of the contemporary statement: We keep only that which we give away.

A Wrenching Farewell (20:36-38)

For all his brave talk about marching steadfastly to Jerusalem, when the final moment of parting came, Paul and the elders were overcome with sadness. They had loved and labored together for years. God had blessed their efforts with much success and had bonded them together with a marvelous friendship. They knew that Paul was right. Never again on this earth would they meet. It was too much. Grown men knelt by the seashore, joined hands, prayed to their heavenly Father, and wept. Then, spent by tears, yet profoundly encouraged by his words and example, those stalwart Ephesian leaders escorted Paul to his ship, and with one more round of desperate, clinging embraces they put him on board and watched him sail away.

Seven Days in Tyre (21:1-6)

Here is a picture of travel by boat in the days of the New Testament, and a more succinct, vivid account is not to be found (vv. 1-3). Paul and his friends traveled for a while by coastal boat that put in at seacoast towns all along the way. Cargo would be loaded and unloaded, passengers taken on and discharged. Only when forced by dire necessity did these boats travel after dark. There were very few lighthouses, and lacking any but the crudest of navigational tools, it was extremely dangerous to sail into the night.

At the town of Patara, the pilgrims were able to book passage on probably a larger vessel that was sailing directly from Asia Minor across the eastern end of the Mediterranean Sea to Phoenicia, which would speed up their trip considerably. When we understand the lack of comfort on these vessels and the crude navigational devices, we can better appreciate the toll that his extensive travels must have taken on Paul and those who journeyed with him.

Though Paul had spent little or no time in Tyre before, he took advantage of the seven-day layover to seek out the Christian disciples of the city, have fellowship with them, and relate to them his experiences as a missionary (vv. 4-6). Most likely, the church in Tyre was made up primarily of Jewish Christians who had been forced to flee Jerusalem after Stephen's death, maybe even running to get away from this same Paul. If that were the case, all animosities had long since been put aside and the two groups made the most of their time together, mutually strengthening each other.

Some among the Tyrian Christians, convinced they spoke through the Spirit of God, tried to persuade Paul from going to Jerusalem, knowing full well the danger that awaited him there. Not wanting to question their sense of leadership by the Spirit, Paul was nonetheless sure that he was being led by the Spirit to Jerusalem.

Another of those warm, touching farewell scenes unfolds as the pilgrim group prepared to board ship and sail away. The Tyrian Christians, newfound friends by now, walked with Paul and his colleagues to the shore and knelt on the beach to pray for God's best to the travelers.

Arrival in Caesarea (21:7-14)

One day's sail down the coast from Tyre lay the port of Ptolemais, the most southern of Phoenician harbors (v. 7). The city is known in the Old Testament as Acco, but its name was changed during the Greco-Roman era to Ptolemais, only to have its ancient name Acco transliterated to Acre during the time of the Christian crusades in the Middle Ages.

The next day the party once again boarded the ship and sailed on to Caesarea (vv. 8-9).

Whatever misgivings Paul may have felt in getting closer to Jerusalem were dispelled by the warmth with which Philip, one of the original seven deacons, and his family received Paul and his group of international Christians. More than twenty years had passed since Philip had been set aside as a leader in the Jerusalem church. After his breathtaking encounter with the treasurer of Ethiopia (Acts 8:26-40) and the evangelistic campaign into Samaria, tradition has it that Philip settled in Caesarea for many years, reared his family, and served his Lord faithfully as an effective leader of the Christian work in that part of Palestine. He must have been an outstanding Christian father to have four daughters who were known for their devotion to the Lord Jesus, as expressed through their chastity and gift of prophecy. They may have helped Luke in filling in some gaps in his understanding of the gospel story. They could have been the ones to tell Luke of their father's ministry in Samaria and to the eunuch.

Here ancient Agabus makes the scene again (v. 10). We first met him when he came to the Christians in Antioch to foretell the famine in Judea (11:27-28). From nowhere, it seems, this old servant of the Lord appears to predict graphically Paul's fate in Jerusalem. Reminiscent of Old Testament prophets, he acted out his message by taking Paul's belt to bind his own feet and declaring, "So shall the Jews at Jerusalem bind the man who owns this girdle and deliver him into the hands of the Gentiles" (v. 11).

When Luke and the others who accompanied Paul heard the dire warning, they tried to dissuade Paul from going any farther (vv. 12-14). This time their pleas and fears almost got to Paul. They may have been voicing some fears he felt. In words like these he pleaded, "Don't do this to me. I have to go. God has ordered me to go. Leave off this crying and pleading. You only make a difficult situation worse. I am prepared to take whatever awaits me at Jerusalem, but you, my friends, must help me by desisting from your moaning."

So be it. With one voice Philip, his family, and all the company who journeyed with Paul declared, "The will of the Lord be done" (v. 14). From here on, all possibility of turning back was gone.

Paul in Jerusalem (21:15 to 23:22)

Hospitality in Jerusalem (21:15-17)

After the stay in Caesarea the pilgrims, along with some members of the local Christian fellowship, prepared for the sixty-four-mile trip to Jerusalem (v. 15). The Caesarean Christians had made housing arrangements for Paul with a man named Mnason, formerly of Cyprus but for many years a resident of Jerusalem and a member of the first Christian group created by the Spirit in Jerusalem. Mnason and his Christian community eagerly, gladly welcomed Paul and his colleagues to Jerusalem (vv. 16-17).

The Jerusalem Elders' Plan (21:18-26)

Since other noted leaders of the Jerusalem church are not mentioned here, perhaps some had died or left the city; but James, the brother of Jesus, had remained to give leadership to the Christian church there (v. 18). Across the years he had gained the admiration and love of the community of faith and the begrudging respect of the Jewish and Roman establishments.

After greeting the respected leaders of the church, Paul proceeded to tell them all that God had done through him for the Gentiles (v. 19). As we have noted before, Paul did not actually owe these elders a report, but out of respect for their position and the position of the Jerusalem church, Paul was willing and eager to relate to them his experiences as missionary to the Gentiles.

Success was his problem. The elders rejoiced over his success, a genuine rejoicing no doubt; then they shared their misgivings (vv. 20-21). Pastor James may have said something like this: "Brother Paul, you may have been too successful. Thousands of Jews have turned to the faith. Many thousands of Gentiles have become followers of the Way. But your success with them has stirred up some animosity among the Jews here in Jerusalem. On top of that, lies have been spread about your work. It is told that you not only release Gentile Christians from circumcision and dietary laws, but you also urge Jews who become believers to relinquish their ancient traditions. We know you do not advocate such practices, but that is the word that has spread like wildfire here in Jerusalem."

To offset the lies and to assure the orthodox Jews of Paul's Jewishness, the Christian elders had devised a plan (vv. 22-24). Paul would accompany to the Temple four Jewish men who had taken a vow of purification and rededication. Paul would go through the same ritual of restoration that the men did and he would pay the Temple fees for the men and himself. This process would take seven days. In this way the Jewish elders hoped the resentment among the orthodox toward Paul would subside.

Paul agreed to this plan. A few years earlier he might have refused to comply, but mellowing and maturity had come to the brilliant, fiery disciple, and he saw the wisdom of the elders' advice.

The conciliar letter that had been constructed out of the Jerusalem conference (Acts 15:1-35) was reissued to Gentile churches (v. 25). It urged Gentile Christians to abstain from meat that had been offered to idols, from blood, from eating meat from animals that had been strangled, and from sexual unchastity. It is interesting and informative to see the equal insistence on all four of these proscriptions.

Paul felt no inner need to go through the Temple rituals; but if it would keep peace in Jerusalem and give him further opportunity to preach to his Jewish brothers, he would spend the time and money to attempt the reconciliation (v. 26). Numbers 6:14-15 indicates that the price for each man would have been two lambs, a ram, bread, cakes, and meat and drink offerings—no mean expense, especially when multiplied by five.

Arrested in the Temple (21:27-36)

It was apparently the last day of the process when some Jews from Asia Minor falsely screamed that Paul had brought a Gentile into the inner court of the Temple (vv. 27-30). Paul had not done such a thing, but truth is often ignored when hatred is running. It is true that Paul had brought Gentiles with him to Jerusalem, but he knew better than to risk his own life and that of his Gentile friends by taking them beyond the Gentile court. All week long Paul and the elders were probably nervous, but every day seemed to bring them closer to safety. It was all over when the mob was aroused. Immediately Paul was seized by the crowd, dragged out of the Temple area, and attacked with stones. It is amazing that he lived long enough for the Romans to rescue him.

Sentries posted at the Fortress Antonia adjacent to the Temple spotted the riot, sounded the alarm, and within seconds a detail of

Roman soldiers, led by the tribune himself, was on its way (vv. 31-36). The anger in the crowd immediately gave way to fear as the spear and sword of the military charged through the mob. Paul was promptly bound with chains and pulled out of the center of the hostile crowd. Probably only when the tribune and his prisoner were on the outer fringes of the subdued but seething mob did the commander stop to ask who Paul was and what this was all about. With one voice the crowd came alive again, hurling accusations and nasty epithets at Paul, probably shaking their fists, and generally making it impossible to get any sense out of the situation. Before further trouble erupted the soldiers and their battered prisoner were ordered to the fortress.

As the soldiers scurried up the steps into the fortress, dragging Paul with them, in Greek the Christian disciple asked permission to address the tribune (vv. 37-40). Astonished that his prisoner knew Greek, the tribune demanded, "Are you not the Egyptian who stirred up the city recently, leading four thousand fanatics off into the wilderness?" "No, I am a Jew, a citizen from the city of Tarsus. And, sir, I wish to speak to the people." Taken aback for a moment the tribune motioned the crowd to be quiet and let Paul stand before them.

Paul's Defense (22:1-21)

When Paul spoke in Hebrew, the crowd grew even quieter so as to hear everything he had to say (vv. 1-5). To be sure, he had not thought it would come under such trying and nearly fatal circumstances, but he had wanted a chance to address his fellow Jews. Paul hoped (even against hope) that his brothers would at last be persuaded that Jesus was the Messiah, and that he, Paul, had simply been carrying out divine orders. With excellent strategy, Paul began his speech by closely identifying with the Jews. Although not of Judah but a Jew nonetheless, Paul was educated under the esteemed Gamaliel, reared in the most orthodox manner, and had vigorously persecuted the new Way when it appeared to be a threat to the ancient religion.

Skillfully he retold his conversion experience on the Damascus Road (vv. 6-16). When the light came, he was knocked to the ground and blinded so that he had to be led into the city. In time, a devout Jew named Ananias, a follower of Jesus, was sent by the Holy Spirit to restore his sight. When healing came, Ananias gave him a warm admonition, and Paul received Christian baptism and became a follower of Jesus.

So far so good; the crowd was listening intently by now. Probably with a silent prayer, Paul moved into the next phase of his sermon (vv. 17-21). He had returned to Jerusalem and started preaching. Then one day while praying in the Temple, he fell into a trance and heard the Lord warning him to get out of Jerusalem because his witness would not be accepted. Although Paul had protested, the Lord had said, "Go to the Gentiles."

The Crowd Explodes Again (22:22-29)

That did it! Just a mention of the word *Gentile* threw the fractious crowd back into an even wilder frenzy (vv. 22-23). Screaming, throwing dust into the air, flailing their garments around, they surged toward Paul and his captors. "Away with him. Death to him. Such a man does not deserve to live."

The entire Gentile issue was a sore spot with the Jews. In the back of their corporate mind they knew they were supposed to be missionaries to the Gentiles, reaching out to draw them into the true worship of Yahweh. But their sense of chosenness and their prejudice that derived from vicious Gentile persecution in the long ago made such a missionary endeavor practically impossible. Paul's declaration that God had called him to preach to the Gentiles rubbed salt into the festering wound of their collective psyche.

Quickly the tribune rushed his prisoner into the fortress for his safety. Determined to get to the bottom of the trouble, the tribune ordered Paul to be flogged into some kind of confession (v. 24).

Once again Paul's Roman citizenship stood him in good stead (vv. 25-29). As the soldiers were lashing him to the whipping post Paul asked, "Is this any way for you to treat a Roman citizen?" Shaken, the centurion in charge of the flogging hastened to the tribune to pass on Paul's question. "Are you a Roman citizen?" the tribune demanded. "Yes," Paul shot back. "I bought my citizenship at a fantastic price; how did you come by yours?" the tribune asked. "I was born a Roman," Paul said. Immediately, his would-be whippers fell back, lest they harm a natural-born citizen of the Empire.

Before the Sanhedrin (22:30 to 23:10)

Determined to learn why the Jews would so viciously attack one of their own and also a Roman citizen, the tribune arranged to have the Sanhedrin convene to hear Paul's case (v. 30). Evidently Rome's philosophy of governing her far-flung empire allowed each country to run its own internal affairs. Only in emergencies did Roman officials step in to have the final word. The tribune would have been content for the Jews to settle with Paul themselves so long as they did not violate his rights as a Roman citizen.

The Sanhedrin was an august body of influential Jews, but Paul was not intimidated by them (vv. 1-5). After all, he knew many of them from his earlier days as persecutor. Also, he had preached to governors, philosophers, and other leaders of men in distant places. So he did not hesitate to address them as "brothers." But that familiarity on the part of the accused along with his poise probably infuriated the high priest, Ananias. He ordered that someone strike the prisoner. He was not above such an act. For many years this cunning man had been a power in Israel either as high priest or as the power behind whomever held the office during a given term. Once he had been summoned to Rome to answer charges of venality but was acquitted and returned home more powerful and ruthless than ever. Records indicate that he was finally deposed in the late fifties of the first Christian century and assassinated in A.D. 66.

In natural anger Paul roared out at the high priest, calling him a bad name. When reprimanded for his insult Paul said, "Oh, I did not recognize him." What exactly did Paul mean by such a statement? The high priest would be hard to miss. Most likely Paul's retort was sarcastic: "I did not recognize Ananias as high priest because a true high priest of God would not stoop to such a vindictive deed."

With another quick statement Paul threw the assembly into a hopeless turmoil (vv. 6-10. He looked at the makeup of the group and saw them to be split between conservative Pharisees and liberal Sadducees. Paul, a Pharisee by birth and training, shouted out, "I am on trial because I believe in the resurrection from the dead." Court for the day was over. Immediately both factions, always spoiling for a fight, anyway, began arguing vociferously. Fearful for the life of his prisoner, the tribune commanded the officers to rescue Paul from them and return to the Tower.

Did Paul deliberately turn the Sanhedrin in on itself? One good look at that hall full of bigoted religionists convinced him that he did not have a chance for justice. Then after the tilt with the high priest, he knew for sure that he had little chance. Wanting to save his life, convinced that God was not through with him yet, he used that rhetorical ploy to have himself rescued by the Romans.

A Fresh Vision (23:11)

Paul must have realized that reconciliation between Christian and Jew was all but impossible, at least in Jerusalem. He had come there with such high hopes. Now after only a few days in the Holy City he had nearly lost his life, and the rupture he had come to heal was even deeper. Also, in calling upon his Roman citizenship to save his life, he had further alienated himself from his strict Jewish brothers. What did it all mean? He had been so very sure that the Holy Spirit was leading him to Jerusalem. All along his route friends had warned him of dire consequences if he came to Jerusalem, all of which had now come painfully true. Apparently, for a day and half he thrashed around in the pits of confusion and despair. By the next night he was utterly exhausted and fell into an uneasy sleep. Then came another of those sustaining visions: "Paul, you are still in my hands," the Lord said. "As you have testified for me in Jerusalem, you shall testify also at Rome."

A Desperate Plot (23:12-22)

But Paul had little respite (vv. 12-15). Forty or more fanatical Jewish zealots bound themselves by an oath neither to eat nor drink until Paul was dead. These vigilantes took the measure of their religious leaders and quickly decided their "spiritual mentors" would cooperate with the plot. The rulers were told to ask the tribune to bring Paul once again to the Sanhedrin so that the case could be settled. But they planned to ambush the prisoner and his guard before they arrived.

But God was still in control (vv. 16-22). At considerable personal risk Paul's young nephew, who had learned of the plot secretly, informed Paul and ultimately the Roman tribune of the black deeds that were being planned.

Next Stop: Caesarea (23:23 to 26:32)

Paul Is Hustled to Caesarea (22:23-35)

Determined not to lose his Roman citizen prisoner at the hands of a crazy Jewish assassination team, the tribune immediately called for two of his centurions (vv. 23-24). He ordered them to muster a large force of men who would escort Paul out of the city under cover of darkness. Paul was to be delivered to Felix, the governor, in Caesarea. The tribune must have felt that things were getting out of hand in Jerusalem, and he wanted his superior to take responsibility for this Jew who was a Roman citizen.

Tribune Claudius Lysias wrote an explanatory letter to the governor so that he could more judiciously dispose of the case (vv. 25-30). This cover letter was sent with the leader of the protective forces. About 9:00 P.M. Paul and his very large escort set out for the seacoast town of Caesarea (vv. 31-35).

Felix was a lucky man. He had the knack for being in the right place at the right time to receive appointments usually reserved for men far above him in birth and station. From A.D. 52 through 59 he ruled the difficult province of Judea in the name of the Roman emperor. Such governorships were coveted, not because of the opportunity for service, but because of the opportunity to line one's pockets with bribes and graft. Felix, though reasonably capable, was not above such practices that would make him rich far beyond his stipend as governor. He finally was deposed and sent back to Rome, being accused of poor administration.

As fitting Paul's rank as a citizen and his reputation as a religious leader, Felix gave him comfortable quarters within the palace, assuring him that the case would be heard as soon as possible.

Another Trial (24:1-23)

With due ceremony, the high priest and some of his colleagues, accompanied by a professional prosecutor named Tertullus, arrived five days later (v. 1). After attempting to ingratiate himself with the governor, Tertullus leveled three charges at Paul (vv. 2-9): (1) Paul was a pest in the empire who stirred up trouble everywhere; (2) he was a leader in the dangerous Nazarene sect; and (3) he was a profaner of the Temple in Jerusalem. Members of the Sanhedrin all concurred in these charges.

In his rebuttal Paul insisted that he had not profaned the Temple; rather, he was quietly going through a process of purification when Asian Jews falsely accused him of defiling the Temple (vv. 2-9). He did not deny, however, his involvement in the Way. Quite to the contrary, he gave a spirited testimony of the power of the Way that had grown out of the Jewish religion. He insisted that he was not repudiating his commitment to the religion of his forebears when he took up the cause of Christ. Throughout his ministry Paul contended that Christianity was the offshoot from the stem of Jesse and David and in no wise a competitor. The reason he was in Jerusalem at this season was the collection and presentation of a love gift to suffering Christians. In closing, Paul declared that the real issue in his trial had been that he had affirmed the resurrection of the dead.

Felix had sat through wordy debates before. Thanks to his Jewish wife, Drusilla, Felix had good understanding of Judaism and evidently of the Way of Christ (vv. 22-23). He also quickly perceived that Paul had done nothing wrong, certainly nothing worthy of Roman punishment. But he also knew that if he summarily acquitted Paul, the Jewish leaders would have a holy fit, stir up a riot, and possibly murder Paul in the process. Under the guise of waiting to talk with the tribune, Lysias, Felix postponed a decision, thanked the Jewish rulers for their time, and ordered Paul placed under a rather loose house arrest.

Private Audiences with Felix and Drusilla (24:24-27)

Why did Felix persist in calling Paul in for private conversations with him and his Jewish wife? Obviously, Paul made both of them uncomfortable as he talked about justice, self-control, and future judgment (vv. 24-25). Still, they invited him on several occasions. It is true that Felix hoped for a bribe, but there must have been something in Paul's message that both attracted and repelled the regal couple. Too bad Felix would not cut loose and fully believe in the gospel. After two years of this cat-and-mouse game Felix was recalled to Rome. To his everlasting discredit Felix refused to release Paul, choosing rather to toss one last bone to the Jewish rulers by leaving Paul under house arrest.

I Appeal to Caesar (25:1-12)

As a direct result of Jewish unrest, Felix was recalled to Rome, being replaced by Porcius Festus (v. 1). Soon after arriving in Judea, the new governor made a "state" visit of sorts to Jerusalem to meet the Jewish leaders and see the Holy City for himself (vv. 2-5). No sooner had he come to town than the Sanhedrin rulers began to apply pressure on the governor to let Paul come to Jerusalem for a trial. These wily elders sought to take advantage of the inexperienced governor. Perhaps Felix had briefed Festus on the Paul issue, or Festus may simply have refused to be stampeded into any action he would later regret. Instead, he invited a representative group to accompany him back to Caesarea, where together they would confront Paul and attempt a disposition of the case.

The entire case had to be reopened to bring the new governor up to date (vv. 6-12). Once again, the spokesman for the Sanhedrin hurled his empty charges at Paul, while offering no proof at all for their validity. For his part, Paul calmly refuted every accusation as it was leveled.

Then the new governor gave the entire situation an unexpected (and providential) turn. Attempting to gain favor with the Jews, Festus asked Paul if he would be willing to go to Jerusalem for a full trial before the Sanhedrin. Paul knew he would have a better chance of survival in a den of hungry lions than he would back in Jerusalem. "I am a Roman citizen being tried before the Roman governor. That's where I belong if I have done anything wrong." Then, taking a deep breath, Paul uttered the words that had tumbled over in his mind often in the years he had endured the palace as a prison, "I appeal to Caesar!"

This appeal was the right of every Roman citizen in Paul's day, though by no means did every citizen in trouble with local law get the privilege of journeying to Rome for a hearing. Festus was elated. He was suddenly off the hook. If he had given in to the demands of the Jews, a miscarriage of justice would have been perpetrated; plus the Sanhedrin would simply have come up with ever new demands on a man they perceived to be a weak ruler. On the other hand, Paul had his friends in high places who would have certainly set up a great noise in Rome if a citizen obviously guilty of no capital crime were turned over to the rapacious mob in Jerusalem. "To Caesar you shall go," Festus declared with a sigh of relief.

God's purposes for Paul were being wrought out, though not at all in the manner the disciple might have wanted. He was on his way to Rome.

Paul and Agrippa (25:13 to 26:32)

Through a very involved course of political intrigue, royal deaths, and bribery in high places, Agrippa, relative of Herod the Great and others of that line, had been made king of certain territories in the northern part of Judea (vv. 13-22). When Festus arrived, Agrippa and his sister Bernice paid him an official welcoming visit. Festus was delighted to see the king, hoping this ruler with Jewish roots would be able to help frame a letter to the imperial courts explaining the Paul problem. During the visit Festus told Agrippa the full story of his trials and tribulations because of Paul of Tarsus. Festus admitted his inability to understand the intricacies of the case and pleaded for King Agrippa's help. Both flattered and curious, the king readily agreed to hear Paul's story firsthand.

The next day, with great ceremony and protocol, the lords and ladies of the city gathered in the courtroom with Festus, King Agrippa and his sister, and certain Jewish leaders to hear Paul's defense (vv. 23-27). When Festus had done with his sonorous intonings, Agrippa gave Paul permission to speak (vv. 1-3). Paul, in turn, declared that he was glad for the opportunity to state his case before the knowledgeable king. Although always pro-Roman, Agrippa had a Jewish background that probably gave him some acquaintance with Jewish religious and political maneuverings. Thus he could listen with some appreciation to Paul's defense. Paul asserted, as he had done before, that he was a son of the Law (vv. 4-11). He did not seek to set aside any of the teachings of the Law; rather he simply wanted to build on them and see them fulfilled in Christ.

Once again Paul retold his own conversion experience on the Damascus Road (vv. 12-18). Notice that each time Paul told the story (or Luke recorded the telling) different shades of the narrative appear, but always there is the consistent theme: original determination to harass Christians; the great light; the voice; blindness; total redirection of his life. Then came his beautiful statement in words like these (vv. 19-23): "I have been faithful to my heavenly vision. I have had help from God. Because of that help I stand before small and great to testify. I say nothing that is not completely in line with what the prophets and Moses taught. I earnestly declare that Christ suffered, died, and was raised from the dead according to God's plan to proclaim light to all peoples."

Evidently Paul's zeal must have compelled the governor to say, "Paul, you are crazy. Your great learning has driven you stark raving mad" (author's paraphrase of v. 24). Not to be turned aside by the outburst, Paul picked up where he left off. Now addressing the king, he bore in on the royal personage (vv. 25-29). Suddenly Agrippa was the defendant. "King, you know what I am talking about; you are alert. These marvelous events have not taken place in a tiny corner. The gospel truth is exploding all over the empire, especially in your kingdom."

"Wait, Paul," the king protested with alarm. "You cannot expect to convert me in such a short time."

But in a final burst of testimony Paul declared, "I wish that all of you were like me—that is, a follower of the Lord Jesus Christ, free in spite of my chains."

All this personal conversation was too much for the royal inquisitors (vv. 30-32). Quickly the king and his sister, along with the governor, swept out of the courtroom. Safely in the governor's chambers, the king and Festus agreed there was no legitimate charge against Paul. If he had not appealed to Caesar he could have been freed. But history's question to them is: In the face of Jewish opposition *would* they have freed Paul?

The Last Stop: Rome (27:1 to 28:31)

Paul Warns of Danger (27:1-12)

As soon as Festus had agreed to Paul's appeal to Caesar, arrangements were made for Paul and some other prisoners to be transported to Rome under the supervision of a centurion of the select Augustan Cohort. Luke accompanied Paul on this voyage. From the seaport of Caesarea, the band of prisoners, their guards, and other passengers took ship on a coastal boat that would put in at the small harbors along the way. The centurion's aim was to sail on this smaller vessel until he could arrange booking on a trans-Mediterranean ship.

After several weeks of slow travel, the desired passage was secured, and the centurion and his group boarded what was probably a large grain ship headed for Rome. The sailing season was getting shorter; the most advantageous time for sailing was late spring and summer. Indications are that it was early fall, which always brought uncertain winds making for slow, erratic sailing. In a harbor of Crete called Fair Havens, a shipboard conference was held with the centurion, the shipowner/captain, and Paul attending. Should they put in here for the winter or attempt to reach a more desirable harbor? Paul, from his years of experience as a traveler, urged them to stop where they were. The centurion and captain, however, wanted to push on to what they regarded to be a safer harbor. Paul predicted that the voyage would be dangerous both to ship and life, but his warning was not heeded.

Into the Storm (27:13-20)

The decision to sail having been made, they still had to wait for a favorable wind that was not long in coming. No doubt with lumps in their throats, the crew headed the ship for the open sea. For a short time all went well, but suddenly a devastating northeaster wind came roaring upon them with no warning at all. Since it was impossible to sail into the wind, the captain was forced to let the ship scud before the gale. After days of this kind of maddening sailing, they managed to put into a harbor of sorts at Cauda where they lashed the ship around with cables to give added strength to the hull. Back into the sea they were driven by the winds, but the storm did not abate. Ship's cargo and gear were gradually thrown overboard, hopefully making the ship more stable in the tossing sea. After days of no relief, crew and passengers began to despair of coming through the storm alive.

Assured by a Vision (27:21-26)

During all these days and nights no one had eaten anything. Who could even think of food while they fought every minute just to stay alive? Then one morning, Paul stood up, clung to a mast or a line, and declared: "We should not have done this. I told you it was a mistake. But take heart. Last night in a dream I was assured that even though the ship and cargo will be lost there will be no loss of life. Take heart. God is not through with me. Because of me you will all be saved."

Shipwreck (27:27-44)

On the fourteenth night of this incredible experience, the sailors sensed they were nearing land. Soundings proved them right. They were drifting toward some unknown island. To slow down the drift, stern anchors were put out. Under the pretense of laying out anchors, some of the ship's crew tried to get into the dinghy, but Paul warned the centurion, "All hands must stay in the boat." The soldiers promptly cut the rope that tethered the small dinghy to the ship. They were now literally all in the same boat.

At dawn Paul urged them to eat some food, and he gave thanks before they ate. Final preparations for beaching the ship were made, only to have their plans dashed when it ran aground at her bow, leaving the stern exposed to the battering of the waves. Quickly, the ship began to break up. On instinct, the guards drew their swords to slay the prisoners lest they escape, but the centurion stopped them and allowed all hands, prisoners included, to get to shore the best way they could. By clinging to floating debris and/or swimming valiantly, everyone made it to safety, fulfilling Paul's prediction.

What an adventure! Paul not only possessed a brilliant mind for fine points of theology and doctrine, but he could be cool and poised under fire. His vibrant faith in God gave him the needed assurance to keep the entire ship's company from despair and/or death.

Wintering in Malta (28:1-10)

In the dawn's early light, natives on the island looked out to the tossing sea and were surprised to see the ship breaking up with its frightened crew jumping overboard, swimming, clinging to planks, struggling for land. By the time the shivering, bedraggled men stumbled to the beach, a big fire was blazing, around which they gratefully hovered, shaking from fear and cold. The island was Malta, off the southern coast of the Italian boot. Luke remembered with deep appreciation the hospitality of the residents of that place.

To keep the fire going, and probably to get his own circulation moving, Paul stirred around the beach, gathering up wood to toss on the fire. Evidently, he picked up a snake, a viper, in some brush, and the fire jarred the snake into lethal activity. To the horror of all bystanders (and probably Paul), the poisonous snake suddenly struck Paul's hand. The natives decided at once that Paul was a murderer who was now being punished by the gods for his evil deeds. But to their amazement Paul suffered no ill effects, and after shaking the snake into the fire he went on about the business of seeing to the needs of the ship's company. The natives' fear quickly turned to awe as the supposed criminal turned out to be a "god."

The governor of the island, a man named Publius, invited Paul, the ship's captain, the centurion, and others among the group to his home, where they were entertained for three days. In the course of the visit, Paul was able to heal Publius' father of fever and dysentery as well as help many others on the island. After three months the weather grew dependable enough for the group to continue their journey on to Rome. Before they left, however, the people of Malta, out of gratitude both for the healing and for the preaching, showered Paul, Luke, and the others with gifts for their voyage

Rome at Last! (28:11-16)

In early February, winter having officially ended for that part of the world, passage was booked on a grain ship that had wintered in Malta. First to the port of Syracuse on the island of Sicily, then on to Rhegium in the toe of Italy, and finally to Puteoli in the Bay of Naples they sailed. For some reason the centurion allowed Paul (probably with a guard) to remain in Puteoli for seven days, during which he and the Christian community there became fast friends and enjoyed a time of mutual deepening of faith.

"And so we came to Rome" (v. 14)! What an understatement. For years Paul had wanted to come to Rome. He had written them, three years before, his great Roman Epistle. He had prayed to see Roman Christians face to face. At long last, after years in prison in Caesarea and one of the most harrowing sea voyages on record, he came to Rome.

Word of his arrival went ahead of him. Imagine his delight and gratitude when he was greeted at two towns along the way by groups of Christians from Rome, some walking as much as forty miles down the Appian Way to greet and make welcome their famous visitor. If the apostle harbored any fears, the sight of those brethren must have completely dispelled them. With tears and embracing, Paul and Luke greeted them. No matter that Paul was a prisoner bound for an uncertain future before Roman courts; he was in the hands of God, and the believers were both honored and delighted to meet him and have him in their midst.

Once in Rome, Paul was again placed under house arrest with freedom to move about within the confines of the residence but without the liberty to leave as he wanted to. Some texts suggest that he was lightly chained to a single guard who was posted to watch him— hence his talk of chains in verse 20.

Paul and the Roman Jews (28:17-29)

After three days for rest and recuperation, he asked leaders of the Roman Jewish community to come to his residence for conversations.

During their visit he explained to them the reason for his imprison-ment. When all the facts were considered, he declared that he was really a prisoner in Rome because of the "hope of Israel." His devotion to the ancient dreams of Israel—of a Messiah and God's intention of a universal brotherhood of believers—had cost him his freedom.

The Jews assured him they had received no communication from Jerusalem about him, and that must have been a relief to Paul. But even more important was their expressed desire to hear more from Paul about the Christian faith, which was gaining momentum in the Gentile world but was still terribly maligned by the Jews. All Paul wanted was an opportunity to preach to them.

On the appointed day a large crowd of Jews gathered at Paul's house to hear him speak. From early morning till late evening he explained the kingdom of God as expressed in Jesus Christ. As he had done all over Asia Minor, he attempted to let them see that Christianity was not a competitor *with* but a fulfillment *of* Judaism. The response was typical—some believed and some did not. Appar-ently to set the record straight, the apostle told the crowd that he was not surprised at the mixed response because the prophet Isaiah long ago had foretold that many of the very ones to whom the Messiah would be sent and from whose nation he would come would reject him. But that would not be the end of the matter. God's salvation had been sent also to the Gentiles, and they would listen.

Epilogue Without a Conclusion (28:30-31)

For two years, at his own expense, Paul lived and preached in Rome, welcoming all who wanted to come to him. We ache to have a defini-tive answer as to what happened to him after the two years. Was he executed? Was he freed? Did he make the trip to Spain he had envisioned? We do not know. But of this we are sure: He preached the unsearchable riches of Jesus Christ openly and unhindered. During those years he wrote his famous "prison epistles," always concerned for persons and churches that were trying to live out the meaning of their faith in Christ.

The book of Acts ends as though there would be a sequel, and that has always been the spirit of the church and the gospel. Thanks be unto God—the story has no end but moves on "unhindered."